America in Crisis

America in Crisis

Glimpses from a Troubled Nation

Dhanpaul Narine

Vitasta

Vitasta Publishing Pvt. Ltd.

New Delhi

Published by
Renu Kaul Verma for
Vitasta Publishing Pvt. Ltd.
2/15, Ansari Road, Daryaganj,
New Delhi - 110 002

ISBN 978-93-80828-04-6

Layout by Vitasta Publishing Pvt. Ltd.
Printed by Vits Press, New Delhi

Contents

Section-III Health and Drugs

Section-IV The Racial Divide

Section-V Economic Indicators

Section-VI Social and Cultural Issues

Section-VII Women and Children

Section-VIII Love, Romance and Sex

Section-IX Entertainment

Preface

In 2005, two events occurred that would lead to the publication of this book. I did not win a seat in the New York City Council. I had some time to contemplate the future. This led to a meeting with Mohamed Alim Hassim, editor of the 'West Indian' newspaper in New York City. Mr Alim thought it might be a good idea for me to write a column for the newspaper. I began to do so, rather tentatively at first, not knowing what the response would be like. However, to our surprise, the articles proved appealing to the readers and there was a demand for more.

The thought then came up that perhaps we should compile some of the articles in the form of a book. As I played around with this idea, a publisher came knocking on my door. Mr Santosh Kumar Verma from Vitasta Publishing in New Delhi, India, had read some of the articles and he was interested in publishing them into a book. The product of our collaboration is "America in Crisis."

Although I take full responsibility for the contents in this book, there are numerous persons to thank for making this project possible. There is Santosh himself, who saw the possibilities of a wide readership when I wasn't so sure. Renu Verma worked tirelessly on the manuscript while maintaining her poise and pleasant attitude. This has made the experience all the more worthwhile.

I have derived tremendous support from my brother Pt. Chunelall Narine, Priest-In-Charge of the Shri Trimurti Bhavan in Queens, New York, and from the Trimurti family as well. My parents Awad and Chandra Narine remain my constant source of inspiration as well as the extended family in Guyana, the United States of America, and Venezuela.

I am indebted to Professor Diane Dittrick for her kind remarks. His Excellency Mr Bayney Karran, Guyana's Ambassador to the United States, and Mr Clem Richardson of the New York Daily News have played important roles and I thank them most profusely. I would also like to thank Shanti Ammar who believed in this book from the outstart and to Mendra Singh for her constant support. One of the objectives of this book is to point out that there is no challenge that is too great and no mountain that is too high to climb. My family members Lionel, Rohan, Sanjay and Miss Sophie strive everyday to make this world a better place and for this I am eternally grateful.

Dhanpaul Narine
September, 2010
New York

Foreword

Making the world a better place has long been a driving force of humankind. In today's world there is an insatiable demand for instant news, which we are able to see with remarkable speed as events unfold. Our lives are filled with images from faraway places and before we can digest them the next tumultuous occurrence competes for our attention. Many of these events are the result of our own handiwork: wars, oil spills, diseases, overpopulation, hunger and the effects of climate change have combined to threaten our very existence. In an incredibly short space of time we have put our planet on the edge of destruction. Now is the time to take stock of what we have done. We need a better understanding as to how to proceed to improve our condition and create a more sustainable way of life.

This book offers ideas and opinions on how we can change our world for the better. Dr. Dhanpaul Narine has written a collection of social commentaries that are timely and relevant. His essays are broad in scope and content. And the topics touch a wide range of subject matter. But whether it's about the crisis in America, democracy in Africa, climate change or women's issues, Dr. Narine shows that we have the potential to make constructive changes that can improve our world. These essays are well written and balanced and the arguments are serious and cogent. One of the many useful qualities of this book is that it is possible to adopt many of the ideas advanced and translate them into practical policy approaches that can ultimately improve our way of living with others and our environment.

Throughout these essays Dr. Narine reinforces the importance of education and learning as a way of achieving social and economic mobility while serving one another and the planet Earth. He points out that there is no gift more precious than education. As we redress the imbalances that beset our world Dr. Narine reminds us that education can provide us with the knowledge needed to transform humanity to the caring society we all seek. He himself has spent his life in selfless service to others and in this volume his humanity shines through like a beacon.

I highly recommend this book to readers and look forward to the next volume.

Diane Dittrick
Senior Associate Laboratory Director
Department of Environmental Science
Barnard College New York, New York

Introduction

America is in a state of crisis. A recent Gallup poll revealed that only 11 per cent of Americans have any sort of confidence in the United States Congress. There is a long list of members of Congress whose behaviors are under scrutiny and who face questions on ethics. In September 2010, unless a deal is struck, the public will get to see the trial of Congressman Charles Rangel who is up for thirteen counts of ethics violation. It will be a most interesting spectacle as the cavalier Congressman attempts to clear his name with the bullish Republicans.

But apart from the ethical and other flaws in Congress, politicians in other fora have not faired well either. In Albany, the capital of New York, there is disenchantment as to how New York State is progressing. Many observers think that the Empire State is not progressing at all. The governor, David Paterson, has to be rated as one of the worst ever in the State of New York. Months have elapsed and when the budget was finally passed there will be a tax on shoes and clothing. This will hurt poor families the most.

This situation is hardly helped by the players in Albany, both in the Senate and in the Assembly, as the debates wither into nothing. There is considerable apathy with the political process in America and those elected are doing little to convince voters that change for the better is around the corner. President Barack Obama talks beautifully but he appears to be handicapped by the will to act decisively. The oil spill problem is still not resolved and immigration is in a mess. Then there are the wars, two of them in far away places.

The Wikileaks showed an America that is badly misled by those on whom support and trust is needed. For example, billions of dollars are given to Pakistan to develop that country and at the same time to enable it to help America fight insurgency. The Wikileaks highlighted a really disturbing picture in which American money in Pakistan may very well used to fight Americans. When asked to explain whether this is the case, the U.S. Secretary of State Hillary Clinton says that, "Pakistan is a complicated country" and that she is reassured by its policies.

The Pakistan ambassador to the United States in buttery language talks about forgetting the past and moving forward. It remains to be seen what form the relationship between Pakistan and the United States will take in the future. The Wikileaks have confirmed what many Americans think: that contrary to the politics as usual the insurgency is a strong as ever and getting stronger with each passing day. On the domestic front, the economy contains to be sluggish, along with rising inflation. But this does not prevent the private sector from awarding itself hefty pay increases, even after Wall Street has stated that the economy cannot afford lavish spending.

These descriptions of corporate impropriety pale into the distance as a continuing saga of the World Trade Center rubble dominate the headlines. In what could appropriately be chronicled as a classic case of American greed the first responders at the World Trade Center (WTC) collapse continue to wait for money that has taken ten years to be approved. Why the delay? The straightforward answer is that the payments are buried in layers of bureaucratic wrangling and partisan politics. When the World Trade Center collapsed, thousands of volunteers went to the site to help. They were motivated by humanitarian concerns. The air was not fit to breathe but try telling that to the government that wanted to open Wall Street for business. The head of the Environmental Protection Agency (EPA)" issued a statement that will long live in the annals of shame. Christine Whitman on September 13th 2001 said, "EPA's greatly relieved to have learned that appears to be no significant levels of asbestos dust in the air in the New York City." This statement was cleared by Condoleeza Rice who was head of the National Security Council at the time.

In the months that followed the WTC collapse there were demands for a public investigation concerning the safety of Ground Zero. The White House in its response decided to classify the documents as secret and President Bush signed an Executive Order to this effect on May 6th 2002. In June 2006, the number of rescue workers who were diagnosed with cancer had risen to 283 persons, 33 of whom had died of the disease.

Some of the disorders included leukemia, lymphoma, tumors of the throat, testicles, bladder, kidneys, intestines and lung. In March 2010, a judge in Manhattan stopped a settlement that would have paid 575 million dollars to the sick victims of Ground Zero. The main reason for his decision was the amount of money that would have been awarded to the lawyers. A Manhattan law firm stood to gain a 40 per cent award that would have amounted to 200 million dollars. But more drama was to unfold and it erupted in Congress.

After years of waiting the first responders and their relatives felt that the Zadroga Compensation Act would finally become law. Passage of the Bill would mean that those who suffered at the WTC site would be entitled to monetary awards, including health care. But the nation was in for a shock and the drama made it clear why America is in a state of crisis. A shouting match between two New York Congressmen held the nation spellbound.

Rep. Anthony Weiner (D) and Peter King (R) traded insults that became political theater at its best. At one point Mr. Weiner refused to yield and that prompted even more outbursts. What are the issues that led to this display of viral venom? At the eve of the debate on the Zadroga Act the Republicans introduced an amendment to prevent the first responders who were illegal immigrants from receiving health benefits. This was not in the original arguments. The majority of these illegals were of Hispanic origin and this would not sit well in Hispanic America, or in the conservative belt. The Democrats saw this as a trap and decided to spring one of their own.

A simple majority would see the Bill through but the Republicans could make all sorts of amendments to it in the process. In order to stop this the Democrats decided to introduce a two-thirds voting stipulation for the Bill to become law without amendments. If the Republicans refused to vote for it they would be seen as heartless. The trap was set. In the end, the Bill was voted down by 35 votes. The tragedy is that most of America want the first responders to benefit from monetary rewards but party politics got in the way.

The will of the people was defeated by partisan politics. Who suffers when this happens? It is those who threw race, religion and politics aside and rushed to save human lives on September 11, 2001.

Section-I

America in Crisis

Chapter-1

The Great 9/11 Cover-up

Denials, cover-ups and bureaucratic bungling. These are all expressions that can be used to describe one of the most inhuman acts of this Century. The towers fell and the dust and smoke melted to become one with nature as all things must. But the terrible impact that this created will be felt for years. As thousands fled from the World Trade Center site, there were those who risked their lives to save others. Firefighters, emergency aid workers and volunteers were on hand in the rescue operation. Many lost their lives in a heroic attempt to find others. But for those workers who survived to tell the tales of that day, it has been mostly a story of horror.

When President George Bush spoke on top of the rubble of the World Trade Center site, it was clear that many workers did not wear masks or any other forms of protection. Thomas Cahill, a professor of Physics and Atmospheric Science, said, "Only 30 per cent of the firefighters working at the site on October 2001 were wearing any protection at all. You had the workers working on top of a huge incinerator in the rush to get Wall Street going again." Air quality experts say that the remains of the World Trade Center acted like a chemical factory that produced and emitted gases, acids and toxic metals for at least six weeks after the explosions.

In an effort to show the level of contamination, the American Chemical Society conducted a research and found that the air quality was indeed poor in the 8,000 air samples collected. It is argued that from the first day of the explosions in Manhattan, there was a calculated attempt to cover up the fact that the fumes were toxic. Wasn't it Christine Whitman who went on television and told the nation that the air at Ground Zero was fit to breathe? Christine Todd Whitman, a former New Jersey Governor, was head of the Environmental Protection Agency (EPA) at the time. The information by Governor Whitman and others led to a number of policy acts. First, by assuring New Yorkers that the air was breathable, thousands changed their plans. It is amazing what one sentence can do. Whitman said on 13 September 2001 that "monitoring and sampling conducted on Tuesday and Wednesday have been very reassuring about potential exposure of rescue crews and the public to environmental contaminants."

This statement was interpreted by the thousands living in and around the WTC site to mean that the air quality was good. But rather than moving out, they remained in their homes and in their businesses. Who gave approval for the statement to be issued? In other words, Christine Whitman had to take orders from someone, a superior sitting in an office somewhere. According to a *New York Post* report in September 2006, the person who gave the final approval for the EPA Press Release was Condoleezza Rice. Ms Rice was at the time head of the National Security Council that had the final say on EPA statements about the quality of air in lower Manhattan.

But what information did the EPA have on the air quality before it issued the infamous statement? According to the *Post*, the EPA had almost immediately concluded that there "were high asbestos levels in the area". Why then, with this information on hand, did the EPA release a statement that the air was fit to breathe? The answer to this question leads to the second reason as to why there was a rush to inform the public that everything was normal. There was Wall Street next door. This is a globally important financial institution and with the World Trade Center gone, getting Wall Street open and working was a top priority. It was a sign of normalcy for a nation that was wounded.

But something was amiss. It is now established that on 12 September 2001, the EPA's own tests revealed that the air was unfit for breathing. However, three days later Christine Whitman was on the airwaves again. She told reporters, "The good news continues to be that the air samples we have taken have been at levels that cause no concern." This was another reassurance that was more specific than the one issued earlier. A day later, Whitman stated unequivocally that "New York is safe".

In the ensuing years, many persons who were the primary or first responders at the WTC site became ill. These internal respiratory illnesses were described as "the World Trade Center cough". In the five years after the tragedy, thousands became ill with various diseases. But it was an uphill battle to convince the authorities that the illnesses were related to the World Trade Center tragedy. In January 2006, this changed.

James Zadroga, who worked at Ground Zero, died. The New Jersey coroner ruled that his death was "directly" linked to

11 September 2001. It was estimated that by April 2006, there were at least 15,000 persons who had medical problems linked to the World Trade Center tragedy. In June 2006, Christine Whitman told the nation that she was proud of the way she handled the WTC crisis. While she was making this statement, the Health Clinic at Bellevue Hospital in New York was treating 1,300 patients for respiratory ailments "that came on or after 9/11 and the number is growing every week". On the Sixth Anniversary of the WTC tragedy, Christine Whitman was interviewed on '60 minutes'. It was clear that she did not want to accept any responsibility for misleading the public. Who was to be blamed for so many people getting sick? She puts the blame squarely on the city of New York which she described as "the primary responder". Michael Cardozo, the city's corporation attorney was stern in his reply. He said, "The city did everything to protect the workers."

The former Deputy Mayor of New York said, "The EPA publicly reported that the general air quality was safe and the city repeatedly instructed workers on the pile to use their respirators." This is a classic case of doublespeak. The EPA is blaming the city, and the city is blaming the EPA while thousands are getting more sick and lacking benefits. It must be noted that the much-hyped Mayor Rudy Giuliani also said repeatedly that the air quality was safe. Where does the truth in all of this lie? Christine Whitman could have done a better job by informing the workers about the hazards of the site.

In her '60 minutes' interview, she said that what she really meant was that the "ambient air around Lower Manhattan was safe" and not necessarily around Ground Zero itself. But playing with words is hardly improving the quality of life for those who are sick. The federal government and the city of New York must take responsibility and pay up those who are suffering. A class action suit is pending in the courts but this will take an eternity before any settlement is made. In the meantime, the city, state and federal government must act quickly to make restitution to those who gave their lives in service to others.

Chapter-2

America's Credit Crunch

They voted against it before they voted for it! In today's economy, things are hard. Credit is frozen. The price of food has doubled. Gas and electricity rates are up and property taxes have also increased. The MTA in New York had announced that it wants to raise fares to plug a budget gap. There is always a 'budget gap' with the MTA while the quality of service gets worse. The simple fact is that it is expensive to live in New York City, and it may not get any better. If you want to buy a car, your credit score has to be above 700 and if you are thinking of buying a house, well, that's another story. In fact, it is the mortgage crisis that have precipitated the biggest financial crisis in America and led to a global crisis. The 700 billion dollars bailout may only be the start of a much bigger package.

While the poor and middle classes are struggling to make ends meet, Richard Fuld, the former CEO of Lehman Brothers, wasn't quite sure whether he walked off with 500 million or 400 million dollars from his company that is now bankrupt. When John Smith worked three jobs to find the down payment for a home, he was led into the den by a pack who had thousands to make. This well-oiled machine comprising real estate agents, brokers and banks targeted innocent families. They couldn't care less whether these families could afford their monthly mortgage payments. In the offices of high finance, deals were cooked up. Who really cared whether John Smith lost his home, as long as the fat cats got their commissions?

But the bubble did burst. Millions of families foreclosed, confidence in banks was crumbled and the result was a crunch of enormous proportions. The biggest culprit in the game was the banks that lent huge sums of money knowing full well that people could not keep up with their mortgage payments. A year ago, most people may not have heard of the term 'credit crunch' but now it has become popular in the lexicon and is used quite frequently in Wall Street and elsewhere.

A 'credit crunch' can be defined as a severe shortage of money or credit. What is the genesis and time line of the crunch and how will the bailout affect ordinary people? The first real signs of the credit crunch began between 2004 and 2006. In this two-year period, the interest rates in the United States rose to 5.3 per cent. The housing market showed signs of contraction and homeowners began to default on their mortgages. In addition, the default rates on sub-prime mortgages reached record levels. Sub-prime mortgages are high-risk mortgages to people with poor or no credit histories.

In April 2007, New Century Financial, a big sub-prime lender, went bankrupt. It sold many of its debts to other banks and it wasn't long before these bad debts began to impact banks around the world. Three months later, Bear Stearns told its investors that little or no profits would be made from its hedge funds. The Federal Reserve Chairman Ben Bernanke said that the US sub-prime crisis could cost up to 100 billion dollars. The banks were too busy giving out loans to lenders.

By August 2007, the European Central Bank was pumping 95 billion euros into the banking market and in the following month, the German lender 1KB announced a one billion dollars loss in investments. Northern Rock in England had to get emergency financial support from the Bank of England to stay in business. A year ago, the Swiss Bank UBS announced a loss of five billion dollars in sub-prime investments. The head of Merrill Lynch resigned at the end of October 2007 after it was revealed that the investment bank lost seven billion dollars in bad debts.

The year 2008 began with a gloomy forecast by the World Bank, and by February, leaders of the G7 said that "worldwide losses that stems from the collapse of the US sub-prime mortgage market could reach 400 billion dollars." This led to the first bailout when the Federal Reserve made 200 billion dollars available to banks to improve liquidity in the markets. JP Morgan Chase purchased Bear Stearns for 240 million dollars but a year earlier Bear Stearns was worth 18 billion dollars.

The summer of 2008 saw the collapse of Fannie Mae and Freddie Mac. They owned five trillion dollars worth of home loans. Both were rescued by the Federal Government. It was one of the largest bailouts in US history. In September 2008, Lehman Brothers were in trouble and in the UK, lender Bradford and Bingley was nationalized. Citi Group agreed to buy Wachovia in the United States and agreed to absorb 42 billion dollars of Wachovia's losses but there was Wells Fargo which also wanted Wachovia. This time line has taken us to the eve of the latest bailout proposals.

Why did the House of Representatives vote against the bailout and what was the motive? Was it politics as usual? According to Barney Frank, a Democrat and head of the House Banking Committee, "It is hard to get political credit for avoiding something that hasn't yet happened." But how will the rescue work? Banks will be required to sell their mortgage-based securities in auctions. Writing the rules of the auctions and hiring private financial firms will take time, maybe at least six weeks. As can be seen, passing the bailout plan is just the first stage.

It may not be palatable to shore up a financial system to avert a crisis with public funds but if the economy is to make a jump start, then this step had to be taken. However, for banks to obtain any relief auctions, they will have to get a price that is higher than 20 cents on the dollar. One way to determine whether the bailout plan is working or not will be to look at what happens to the rate the banks charge each other for borrowing money. This is known as inter-bank rates. According to one economist, "The banks don't want to lend other banks when they don't know what toxic assets they may be holding."

How will new cash flow into the system? This will depend on whether or not the auctions help to put a reasonable price on the toxic debts and take them off the balance sheet of the banks. Assuming that this happens, inter-bank rates would fall and the flow of credits will be eased throughout the economy. John Smith will then be able to get a loan from his local bank to buy a car, or to secure a mortgage on a house with proper oversight.

Chapter-3

Financial Downturn

In a bright and cheerful real estate office sits a broker and a client. The paperwork is being filled up for a mortgage. The client loves the house and the broker wants a sale. The snag is that there is no way that the client can afford the house with his income. But a sale is a sale and the broker is aggressive. By doctoring the books to show inflated incomes for the client and his unemployed wife, and using his contacts in the banks, a mortgage is approved. This has been part of the game that is well understood by many brokers, banks and attorneys for years.

Recently, these corrupt practices have been exposed, especially when buyers have begun to fall behind payments and lose their homes. The economic downturn with a weakening dollar and rising prices have led to a situation in which mortgages cannot be repaid. There simply isn't much money earned by families to make ends meet. When one or two clients face foreclosure, it could be part of the normal operations of the market. It represents only a tiny drop in the financial bucket and steps would be taken to correct any default loans by banks.

But what we have seen in the recent past is not the occasional or normal foreclosure. Countrywide, there have been foreclosures in thousands. This means that the banks are losing millions of dollars and the housing market is depressed. What has led to this situation and what options do the banks have at the moment? A New Yorker bought seven houses in Orlando, Florida for investment purposes. But, tenants of five of the houses moved out. They could not afford the rents anymore. The tenants of the other two houses refused to pay the rent or to move out and they are facing legal proceedings.

In any case, the landlord has to fork out the mortgage on the seven houses every month with no income being generated from them. The landlord has put the five houses for sale but no offers have been made. He is now struggling to pay the mortgage and recently he made a decision to stop payment. He would "let the banks do whatever they want." Those seven properties are worth over two million dollars. The banks have to bear the loss and millions of such cases nationwide.

This anecdotal reference highlights the mess Americans face as the country grapples with a recession that is as big as the last Depression. It has long been the view that America is a nation of debt. For instance, foreign banks own 1.5 trillion dollars from mortgage giants Fannie Mae and Freddie Mac. China, the Middle East and Russia have around 700 billion dollars in debt that they owe America and which they cannot repay. When this happens, the cost of living of Americans rise and standards of living fall.

In 1938, Fannie Mae was founded by President FDR Roosevelt to provide liquidity to the mortgage market. Today, Fannie Mae and Freddie Mac own almost half of all home loans in the United States. When millions of homeowners foreclose, these institutions face billions of dollars in losses. The sub-prime crisis last year affected many people in many states. In a six-month period, the construction industry folded in some parts of America.

For example, in Rhode Island, those who were involved in construction lost their homes because no new houses were built between November 2007 and March 2008. In Missouri, families were behind in their mortgage payments after they lost their jobs and the same applies to North Carolina and other states as well. How is the inability to repay ones mortgage related to Fannie Mae and Freddie Mac?

Most home mortgage lenders depend on these two giants to provide the funds. They are big on the Wall Street as other banks do business with them and as we have seen other foreign countries have billions of their funds tied up in debt securities. According to the *New York Times*, "There is a real panic on the Wall Street right now and sometimes a blaze like that grows almost without reason. There wasn't really any new news to set off this crisis. The stocks just started falling and did not stop." About a year ago, the shares of Fannie Mae and Freddie Mac were trading at 60 dollars, but this has dropped by over half since.

America was stunned when there was 'a run on the bank.' While the government was trying to reassure the country that Fannie and Freddie were healthy, IndyMac customers thought differently. Bancorp, a huge mortgage leader, collapsed and the Federal Deposit Insurance Corporation (FDIC) set up a new bank to oversee IndyMac's assets. IndyMac has had a ripple effect in the finance industry. Wachovia, the fourth largest lender in the US, tried to allay the fears of its borrowers only to find its shares sinking further.

The lesson from IndyMac is that no bank is too big to fall. Once public confidence is eroded in a banking institution collapse is imminent. Another lesson is that funds for ailing banks are not limitless. IndyMac was good in getting customers by offering attractive interest rates but once this profile was in crisis, there was a 'run' on the bank. But the financial crisis has been the subject of several 'spins' for some time now. The government has tried to put a brave face on it.

According to the *Economist*, "Falling real incomes, slumping shares and house prices and tighter credit all cast a cloud over consumer spending. The Fed's trouble is that, though the economy has avoided recession so far, it may not do so for much longer."

However, there are other areas that have to be looked at as well. The tax relief in stimulus package had only a short-term impact. The construction industry experienced only a temporary upswing. The vacancy rates for office and commercial space has hit rock bottom and retail chains are closing, with Starbucks and the Gap being among them. The second point is that consumer spending has dropped. The tax rebates saw an increase in consumer spending. But the rebate came at a time when food prices had increased and so had the prices for basic utilities including gas. The economy then was hardly stimulated by a one-off payment.

The final area concerns home equity loans. As banks cut mortgage, refinancing more homeowners turned to borrowing against the equity of their homes. But care has to be exercised here because it is so easy to fall to the temptation of easy money. What is the best possible hope to get out of the mortgage crisis? The short-term solution depends on increased local production and a strong overseas market.

But if inflation rises, interest rates may have to be raised soon.

Advice has come from an unexpected source. Yoshimi Watanabe, Japan's Financial Services Minister, has recently spelled out what America can do to stem the crisis. Writing in the *Financial Times,* he said, "It is essential for the US to understand that given Japan's lesson, public fund injection into the financial sector is unavoidable." Public funds will undoubtedly be injected into Fannie Freddie and interest rates will increase, leaving the lower and middle class to bear the brunt of the hardships.

Chapter-4

Teenage Pregnancies

We live in an age of the unwed mother. It is Friday night in New York City. There are long lines on the sidewalk. Teenagers have been waiting for hours. The clock strikes midnight and the doors are open. The nightclubs will soon be filled with teenagers partying the night away. Where are the parents when this is happening? At the risk of asking the obvious question: what time will these teenagers get home and will there be any consequences?

In fairness, the nightclubs do not force anyone into their premises and adults enter as a result of free choice. It is undeniable, however, that the time has come for us to revisit and examine the reasons as to why so many of our teenagers are led astray and why many young girls are left literally holding the baby. It should be made clear that this article does not seek to condemn but to suggest options that young people can use to pursue healthy lifestyles. When Governor Sarah Palin told the world that her daughter, Bristol, became pregnant at 17, it led to an avalanche of criticisms from the media and the community. It also opened up a much-needed debate as to how our society is treating our teenagers and what can be done to involve them productively.

In New York City, the statistics concerning teenage pregnancies are hardly comforting. In 2006, there were 7,646 teenage pregnancies in Brooklyn. This was followed by 6,510 in the Bronx; 4,688 in Queens; 3,359 in Manhattan and 897 in Staten Island. This amounted to over 21,000 teen pregnancies for New York City alone. What is even more shocking is that 7,000 students gave birth while they were enrolled as students in New York public schools.

How many fathers stood by their girlfriends is not quantified but anecdotals from teens themselves cast evidence on the heartaches and disappointment of those who have failed to achieve their goals. One young woman said, "It's hard being a teen mom. The responsibility is enormous. One moment you are free and then there is another life to look after. You can't think about yourself anymore."

Another young lady who became pregnant at the age of 17 felt that she had let down all those who had confidence in her. She pointed out that "getting pregnant at the age of 17 was the worst thing that could've happened at the time. My parents went off the handle when they found out. They had invested so much in my education and now I couldn't graduate from college. My education was put on hold. I was attending one of the most expensive private schools at the time."

The stories may have been different but for most teenage pregnancies, there is a combination of disappointment and unfulfilled dreams. Some parents tend to feel that the pregnancies of teenagers are their fault. They should have seen the warning signals, communicate more with their daughters, or just do something to help their children.

The age of the unwed mother has led to the concept of "children having children" and this has fueled a public sense of crisis. It is important to look at teen pregnancies from two different levels to get some measure of the scope and impact of the problem. The first is to examine the nature and extent of teenage pregnancies in New York while the second is to compare statistics between the United States and the rest of the world. New York City has a pregnancy rate that doubles the rest of the state while the United States leads all industrialized nations in teenage pregnancy rates. The Guttmacher Institute finds that "teen pregnancy rate in the US is almost twice that of Great Britain and Canada, and four times that of Sweden and France."

These statistics are interesting but may prove to be of little comfort to parents in New York who have teenagers. What about the sexual activity of teenagers and to what extent is any form of birth control used? According to a New York City Department of Health Report, "Nearly half of public high school students in New York City and nationwide say that they have indulged in sexual activity." The report states further that 41 per cent of ninth graders and 58 per cent of twelfth graders are currently sexually active and about 1 in 10 has had sex before the age of 13. The effect of such sexual activity can have devastating effects. Sexually transmitted diseases (STDs), such as Chlamydia, can cause infertility and other serious health problems. In addition, teenage parents are less likely to complete high school. Their children can have low birth rate, suffer from behavior disorders and become the victims of child abuse and be trapped in poverty. Teen mothers too are prone to emotional problems and stress.

The use of contraceptives is not widespread among teenagers. In the South Bronx, "Twenty-six per cent of teenage girls are most likely to report having sex without birth control," according to a recent report. The knowledge of contraceptives varies by borough in New York City. However, a high percentage of teenagers stated that they know about the various forms of contraceptives that exist, but the use of them is infrequent. For example, among sexually active teenagers ,16 per cent say they have ever been pregnant or gotten someone pregnant.

What about abortions? The percentage of spontaneous and induced abortions is high especially among blacks and Hispanics. It was nearly five percent per 1,000 and that was much higher than the one per cent when compared to whites. Two other factors are worth mentioning. The first is previous pregnancy and the second is the extent to which teenagers have financial coverage. In New York City, 33 per cent of teenagers who had a live birth had been pregnant once before and among these 52 per cent had a child from a previous pregnancy. Overall, 80 per cent who had a live birth used Medicaid as their main form of payment.

As a society, what can we do to encourage our teenagers to stay on the right path? There are a number of suggestions that have been advanced to help teenagers develop and practice healthy behaviors. The school system is perhaps the most important institution along with the family that can help to reinforce and change behaviors. The schools need to do more through its counseling and peer intervention programs to bring into purview the hazards of teenage pregnancies. Lectures by prominent individuals and by teens who have experienced pregnancies can also bring home the problems associated with pregnancies at an early age.

A child is the product and reflection of the family. It is therefore fitting that much of the day to day counseling is done in the family. The initial accent should be on cultivating healthy relationships by highlighting the positive aspects of schooling and education. When schools and families work together, the chances are that the child will grow up well rounded and see the world through positive lens.

Sex education is an inescapable fact of life. It is suggested that health care providers should document the sexual history of their adolescent patients and offer them advice and health services. But we cannot leave it only to the providers. Parents, churches, community leaders and schools also have a role to play in the education of teenagers about premarital sex, unwanted pregnancies, diseases and contraceptives.

One of the most effective ways to prevent teenage pregnancies is to create avenues for parents and their children to communicate with each other. In addition, opportunities for teenagers to develop social skills, vocational competence and artistic and athletic talents should also be encouraged. There is no one who can provide all the solutions to teenage pregnancies, but as can be seen, if a community pools its resources and works together, our young people will be busy doing the right and positive things.

Chapter-5

A World of Drugs and Money

When the summer light fades, the doors to another world are opened. At street corners, young men and women know the signs. A nod or flick of the fingers can mean a drug sale is imminent. It doesn't have to be in pounds or kilos. A little plastic bag of marijuana or crack/cocaine can fetch between five and twenty dollars, depending on its strength. These 'little plastic bags' litter many streets in New York City. They signify the growing sign of a society that is unable to control the demand for hard drugs. In a good many cases, the selling and use of drugs take place in broad daylight. It appears that society has become numb to the fact that drugs are a part of life.

According to the World Drug Report of 2007, the "use of marijuana and cocaine among eighth grade students doubled between 1991 and 1994, with average age of initiation into marijuana use at 13.9 years." This is a disturbing figure. Can the future be bright and rosy for children who take drugs? The answer is of course in the negative but it begs other questions. How effective is parental guidance and supervision concerning drug use? What are schools doing to fight the menace of drugs?

Saturday nights are a good indicator of a society that lacks the will to impose standards on the young. The nightclubs are open at midnight to long lines of young men and women who are keen on having a rollicking good time. The parties finish at six the following morning. Where are the parents when hundreds of young people are away from home unsupervised?

There are a number of theories concerning the use of illicit drugs. It is pointed out that drug use or psychoactive substances have been around since ancient times. Drug use may be associated with boredom, depression, poverty, heredity, stress or anxiety. But scholars argue that interpretations of drug use ought to focus not so much as to why individuals are drawn into drug use but to look at why people abstain from using drugs. Despite the theories and presuppositions, the reality may be banal. This leads to the discussion as to what is the state of drug use on a worldwide basis.

In Asia, it is estimated that drug use is on the increase and so is the HIV/AIDS epidemic. In Pakistan, a survey was conducted in 1993 on drug abuse. It was found that there were three million drug users of which 51 per cent were taking heroin.

Pakistan is seen as a significant producer and transit point for opiates and cannabis products. In 1992, illicit drug exports by Pakistan accounted for two billion dollars.

In other countries, the supply is also on the increase. Colombia expanded areas of cultivation for heroin from 12,000 hectares in 1990 to 45,000 hectares in 1995. In Italy, the number of drug addicts stands at 100,000 persons while in Sweden, infecting drug users is increasing by 10 per cent annually. The Netherlands continues to be the main source of amphetamines for Swedish trafficking but an increasing amount is being supplied by Poland as well.

The United Kingdom has revealed that 16 to 29-year old who took illicit drugs in 1991 has now doubled. The Home Office reported that the number of drug addicts in Britain doubled between 1990 and 1994. The United States has always been a big market for drugs. Efforts have been made to reduce consumption by deploying more personnel to seize consignments. The most widely used drug in western countries is Cannabis although there was an eighth-fold increase in the use of Ecstasy between 1990 and 1994. In Thailand, about 45,000 addicts are reported each year and they fall into the 20 to 35-year old age group. Drug manufacturing and trafficking are active in Myanmar, Laos, and Thailand, the areas known as the Golden Triangle.

How does Canada fare in the drug world? Canadians use marijuana four times the world average. Recent figures show that 16.8 per cent of Canadians in the 15 to 65 age group smoked marijuana. The world average is 3.8 per cent. The use of heroin, amphetamines and ecstasy is also high in Canada.

What lessons can be learned from the proliferation of drugs worldwide and what are the implications for policy? The first point is that the world is awash with drugs and the supply or consumption is not confined to the industrial rich countries. There are enormous amounts of money to be made from drugs. The Geopolitical Drugs Watch (GDW), based in Paris, stated that drug traffickers are a part of economic globalization. This makes money laundering easy. In 2000, about 400 billion dollars of drug money was reintegrated into the economy.

Africa has a high degree of money laundering where goods are bartered for drugs. Criminal organizations in Europe are using the Pacific Islands as a money laundering paradise. The drug cartels are known to invest money in diamonds, gold, and coffee and cocoa. But the drug tentacles extend much further than in mining and agriculture. These days drug money has infiltrated the military as well as the higher strata of government.

It is no secret that highly placed officials in governments can be bribed by drug cartels to turn a blind eye to shipment and distribution. One of the warring separatist groups in Europe has boosted its coffers through arms and drug dealing. The group boasts of an annual budget of 15 billion dollars. A member of the group point out that, "One day you are told: I will sell you 50 Browning guns but you have to buy a kilo of heroin. It's a big ethical problem. But there are people who depend on you because they have a war to fight."

What can be done to stem the flow of drugs and wipe out the menace completely? The rich countries have increased security measures including seizures and imprisonment. These can be effective but they are only half-way measures. The policy must be to stamp out illicit drugs at the roots. In order for this to take effect, rich countries should encourage poor drug producing countries to diversify their economies. Monetary and technical skills should be offered for the first few years to bring them on stream. But education is the key. More information on the damaging effects of drugs at the primary school level can go a long way to combat the spread of drugs in our communities.

Chapter-6

Too Many Guns on the Streets

In 1982, two youths bought a rifle and decided to test it. They stood on top of a building in Coney Island in New York and fired the weapon. A 45-year old woman was killed as she walked with her son along the street. This prompted the City's Commissioner of Probation to state, "Guns have never been more available or affordable in New York." The rifle that took the lady's life was bought for 80 dollars. In 1981, the police confiscated more than 19,000 illegal guns and the year before the number was around 18,000. Most of the illegal guns, it would appear, were smuggled into New York from states where no permit is needed. People in those states can purchase guns by merely showing a driver's license with a local address.

The Deputy Inspector of the 60th Precinct, said that "whenever you have a drug problem, you have a gun problem." What was alarming in the shooting of the lady was the fact that a rifle was used, since most of the guns in the streets are handguns. As one teenager in Brooklyn said, guns are everywhere. In Brighton Beach, rifles could be bought for as less as 15 dollars. What has really changed in the last 25 years? How effective are the gun laws in New York and have they been able to stem the tide of gun violence?

The statistics show that there were 14,659 violent crimes committed with guns in New York in 2001. Who were arming the criminals? According to the County Sheriff for Albany, "Something's not working, because there are too many guns on the streets." He pointed out that this wasn't due to the fact that there were no gun laws in New York. In fact, New York has some of the strictest laws in the nation but the problem is that guns can easily enter New York from other states.

A report titled 'Americans for Gun Safety' submitted in 2002 stated that guns in New York are stolen at a rate that is about one quarter of the national average. The division of Criminal Justices Services, on the other hand, points out that criminal charges for selling guns to a criminal in New York are rare. In 2003, 16,493 guns were seized by the police in the state of New York. What is striking is that most of these guns were used in crimes. How many persons were charged out of the 16,000 odd guns that were seized? It boggles the mind to learn that only 57 persons were charged, and out of this number, only 37 were convicted. Clearly, the system is not working.

The proliferation of guns on the streets has not bypassed the Caribbean community. In 2005, a police officer of Jamaican origin was allegedly murdered by a Caribbean immigrant. Nick Perry, the New York Assemblyman said at the time, "The shooting death of Dillon Stewart should remind all of us that too many guns are in the hands of people who shouldn't have them." Mr Perry blamed several places for the increase of guns on the streets, including Washington. Yvette Clarke, who was a Councilwoman at the time, said that more aggressive action was needed to reduce the number of guns in the hands of criminals. Dr Kendall Stewart, a Councilman in Brooklyn at the time, called for gun control laws at the federal level to be toughened.

It was, however, Mr Perry who made the most telling observation. He called on Washington to take steps to limit the flow of weapons from the United States to the Caribbean. Gun related violence is up in the Caribbean, Mr Perry said. He continued, "Certainly, the United States can take stronger measures to crack down on the society of criminals who export guns to our part of the world. These weapons are like a scourge. We don't manufacture guns in New York City or in the Caribbean and all we are hearing is the right to bear arms." New York City has recently hit the headlines in a number of publicized cases in which guns were used to cause mayhem.

Mayor Michael Bloomberg and Reverend Al Sharpton, at a rally in Manhattan, called for an end to the flow of guns on the streets. Mr Bloomberg pointed out that in the last three months, 40 illegal guns were seized. The Mayor also said that two persons were charged in connection with an illegal gun trafficking ring from Florida to New York. The examples of gun violence hit really hard when they are ripped from the headlines. Who can forget Vada Vasquez, the 15-year old student from the Bronx? Vada was returning from school when another teen pulled the trigger that exploded her brain.

At rallies in Manhattan and in the Bronx, New Yorkers called for an end to street violence and an end to streetcorner thuggery. One substitute teacher appeared to sum up the situation most succinctly when he said, "People are sick and tired of opening up the *Daily News*, listening to the TV and seeing innocent people being shot, murdered or attacked for nonsense, for silliness." In Times Square, some protesters called guns the new crack as guns are undermining the quality of life in the neighborhoods.

But as the city expresses its outrage, there is news that guns in other states are being sold openly and they are tax-free as well. According to a report published in the *Daily News*, South Carolina heads the five states that provide 85 per cent of the illegal handguns that are recovered in New York City. It was further reported that South Carolina were selling guns tax-free during the Black Friday holiday. The gun shops there were expecting a big jump in sales.

In order to see the deadly effects of guns, one only has to read the papers on a Monday morning. The horrible statistics and descriptions of gun-related incidents are there in bold print. For instance, one newspaper published the story of a man who walked into a coffee shop in Washington and shot four police officers dead, and for no apparent reason. The officers were working on their laptops when the man gunned them down. A statement from the Sheriff's office said, "We have no motive at all for the deaths of these officers. I don't think when we do find out, it will make sense." The man in question was shot by the police a few days later.

In New York, a teen from the Bronx was shot to death three blocks away from his home. Meanwhile, in Staten Island, a gang war turned bloody, killing four people in November 2009. This prompted the Staten Island District Attorney to remark, "This violence must and will stop. Reporting someone who has an illegal gun is not snitching. It may avoid the tragedies we have seen in other boroughs where innocent victims were struck by stray bullets."

Given the number of unlicensed guns on the streets and the incidence of violence on a daily basis, there is an urgent need for action to restore law and order. What can be done to keep our streets safe? There are calls for regular police patrols and the involvement of community leaders. Both of these are good suggestions as is an amnesty. But the real strategy must begin with education that includes parental responsibility and community policing.

Chapter-7

Divorce in America

Breaking up is easy to do. When parents divorce, children suffer. The first marriage took place in America in 1621. A magistrate performed the ceremony and the injunction was stated clearly: what God has put together, let no man rent asunder. But the flesh is weak and the first divorce in America took place in 1639 when Mrs James Luxford found out that her husband was also married to another woman. The man was fined 100 pounds and banished to England as punishment. By 1850, the divorce rates in the United States had risen to the point where it was among the highest in the world. Today, divorce is so rampant that marriage as an institution is crumbling, according to many sociologists.

A number of studies have revealed that 50 per cent of all marriages in America end in divorce. But the Institute of Professional Psychology shows that the figures for second and third marriages are even more devastating. The divorce rate for second marriages is 60 per cent while that for third marriages is 73 per cent. The divorce rate for childless couple is higher than that of unions in which there are children. According to researchers, the absence of children leads to loneliness and weariness, and at least 66 per cent of all divorced couples in United States are childless.

In America today, breaking up is easy to do and it is done with alarming regularity. The Heritage Foundation states that "each year, over one million American children suffer a divorce of their parents; more over, half of the children born in 2010 to parents who are married will see their parents divorced before they turn 18." The effects of divorce and a broken home are many and are viewed mostly in negative terms. In other words, social scientists are finding it difficult to come up with good reasons for couples to get a divorce.

Every marriage is different but some of the reasons for divorce remain the same. A lack of communication between spouses, money problems, and infidelity are the main factors that contribute to the breakup of marriages. Commitment in a marriage requires hard work and the ability to make compromises. The United States has the highest divorce rate and also the highest rate of solo parenting in the world. Some relationship experts feel that "society has changed from the importance of the family to the importance of me. The attitude seems to be that if the marriage doesn't work, I can get a divorce because it is easier to fill out paper work than to put in the time and effort to make the marriage work."

What are some of the effects of divorce? It is argued that children become the victims of abuse and tend to experience traumatic and emotional problems. A child whose parents have been separated is transformed from a happy person to one who is withdrawn and uncommunicative. This behavior affects the child's performance in school as well. Children who are from divorced parents tend to perform below par in the key subject areas such as reading and math. Truancy and drop out rates from school cannot be ruled out either.

In New York, life in the inner city shows that a significant proportion of households are affected by divorce. Children are raised by a single-parent or grandparents. There is considerable neglect in the upbringing of children and this leads to the lack of a decent family life. Researchers point out that the divorce of parents, "even if amicable, tears the fundamental unit of society. Families who were not poor before their divorce see their income drop as much as 50 per cent. Almost 50 per cent of parents with children who are going through a divorce move into poverty after the divorce."

The impact of divorce on the family has been well established. But one area that should get the attention of policy makers is that of delinquency and education. Robert Sampson from the University of Chicago found that "the divorce rate predicted the rate of robbery in any given area, regardless of economic and racial composition." The upside of this is that low divorce rates often result in more formalized networks and lower crime rates. Divorce creates anxiety among children and can disrupt their learning process. As a pre-condition to learning, a stable family life is always preferred.

What about the economic impact of divorce? It has been stated that divorce can lead to diminished incomes. When one working parent leaves the family, incomes are reduced and standard of living falls. When a family cannot afford to live at a certain standard because of separation, it creates feeling of desperation, anxiety, rejection, and depression. There is a conclusion in some studies that when parents divorce, they are, in effect, divorcing their children as well. Divorce can be self-perpetuating and it is likely that in some instances divorce or unstable relationships may occur when the children of divorcees get married.

What can be done to make marriage into a stable and lasting institution? In a recent report in New York's *Daily News*, it was stated that "no fault divorce will be approved by Albany." The Bill has been passed by the Senate and has found approval in the Assembly as well. New York was the 50th state to allow people to divorce without the consent of a spouse or proof of fault. Many organizations are still opposed to the passage of this legislation for fear that the law will open the floodgates to more divorces. Is a happy home life possible, given the pressures that exist?

Divorce pitches children into a battle that few of them really understand. But divorce can be prevented and happiness is possible in many homes. After all, we know people who have been married for years and they really enjoy each other's company. There is no magic formula for a happy married life but some simple common sense approaches can help from seeing the divorce attorney. Each person is unique but criticisms and nagging can be harmful to the relationship. Be patient, tolerant, and use kind words to each other and your marriage will last long.

Praise is indicative of appreciation. Most people want to be told that they are doing a great job. A little thoughtful appreciation goes a long way whether it is in helping to prepare a meal, or to finding out how the day was spent. Courtesy too is an important factor in relationships. One should never hesitate to show courtesy and respect. Politeness is not a sign of weakness but is a reflection of character and good upbringing. It costs nothing to say 'please' and 'thank you' or in holding the door for the person behind you. These little acts of kindness will get you far in life.

Ego and pride are destructive and should be avoided at all costs. Acting mean and 'hard' is not a sign of strength. It puts people off and is often interpreted as being abrasive. Marriage is about compromise, forgiveness and caring. When these are put into action daily, divorce cannot raise its ugly head. So plan a date, dress up for each other and spend time together. It will do wonders for your marriage.

Chapter-8

Medical Malpractice

Medical malpractice has led to a litigation explosion. Doctor negligence and high insurance costs have for long engaged the attention of the medical, legal and insurance fraternity. What exactly are some of the issues involving medical malpractice? Frank Sloan and Lindsey Chepke in their book *Medical Malpractice* argue that the medical malpractice system in the United States is not effective. According to the writers, malpractices do not compensate victims fairly or prevent injuries caused by medical mistakes. The 'Doctors Company', which is a physician-based insurance company, found that wrong site surgery accounted for only five per cent of medical mistakes between 2004 and 2006.

The Comptroller of New York in his annual report stated that for the year 2008, two hospitals had significant increases in medical malpractice claims. According to the report, "Medical malpractice claims filed against Coney Island Hospital rose from 45 in FY 2003 to 60 in FY 2004. Claims against Elmhurst rose from 50 in FY 2003 to 64 in FY 2004." The amount of money paid out in New York in 2008 exceeded 500 million dollars. Clearly, there needs to be some analysis of medical malpractice and even more urgent need for policy reforms.

When sensational headlines flash, the medical profession is viewed negatively and dedicated doctors, nurses, and other staff are tarred with the same brush. There are thousands of doctors, nurses and related staff who care for their patients, make follow-up calls and have an excellent bedside manner. For them, money is secondary. It is patient's care that really matters. These professionals should be saluted. However, there a few who sully the Hippocratic Oath through negligence, selfishness and plain egoism. A few months back, the New York *Daily News* carried an article 'Abandoned in OR' that highlights the need for reform in the system.

The newspaper stated that "two of New York's highest paid surgeons have been suspended for abandoning a patient in the operating room after she was anesthetized and prepped for brain surgery." The doctors in question work at North Shore University Hospital and are considered "stars" in their field. Their salaries command star figures as well. Why then would they abandon a patient who is about to have an operation? The doctor who was scheduled to perform the operation was nowhere to be found. But there was another doctor who could have operated. He refused because it was not his patient. Both surgeons have been suspended indefinitely.

The statistics on medical malpractice are far from comforting in a country as advanced as the United States. An article published in the *Journal of the American Medical Association* (JAMA) states that medical malpractice has become the third leading cause of deaths in the United States, after heart disease and cancer. The journal further stated that there are "12,000 deaths a year from unnecessary surgery, 7,000 deaths from medication errors in hospitals, 20,000 deaths from other errors in hospitals, 80,000 deaths a year from infections in hospitals and 106,000 deaths a year from non-error, adverse effects of medication."

This means that there are over 225,000 people who die each year from 'Med-Mal'. The signing of a consent form does not mean that health care providers are given a license to commit a malpractice. Two of the most publicized cases of medical malpractice occurred in 2002 and 2003 and they will have implications for policy for many years. These case relate to the treatment of Jeanella and Jesica.

In July 2002, Jeanella received a transplant of part of her father's liver at the Children's Medical Center in Dallas. It was alleged that a surgical mistake had destroyed her liver in an earlier operation. In 2002, the doctors thought her father's blood type was a good match when in fact it was the mother's. A mix-up in the laboratory led doctors to give Jeanella her father's blood. This mismatch led to her death on 6 August 2002. Next year, Jesica was the victim of another case of medical carelessness.

Jesica Santillan was born in a poor Mexican town and when she became ill, she was smuggled into the United States by her parents for medical treatment. Jesica's case became well known in North Carolina and the community there raised thousands of dollars for a heart and lung transplant. Jesica received her transplant at Duke University Hospital in February 2003 but a mistake was made when she received the wrong blood type. Her body rejected the new organs. The North Carolina community then mounted a vigorous campaign to find a second compatible heart and lungs. Jesica died two weeks later.

The Los Angeles Times pointed out that medical malpractice caused in these cases by a lack of communication are all too common in medicine. The Federal Agency for Health Care Research and Quality stated, "There is more double checking and systematic avoidance of mistakes in Starbucks than at more health care institutions." *The New England Journal of Medicine* reported that "only 30 per cent of patients harmed by a medical error were told of the problem by the professional responsible for the mistake." This means that 70 per cent had no idea that a mistake was made in their procedures.

Despite these high profile cases, there is a view that because we live in a litigation society, people will sue doctors and hospitals for just about anything. The former President of the United States George W Bush described such legal actions as "junk lawsuits". He argued that medical malpractice lawsuits contributed significantly to the high cost of health care in the United States. The American Medical Association (AMA) makes a most interesting point. It stated that "America's patients are losing access to care because the nation's out of control legal system is forcing physicians in some areas to retire earlier, relocate or give up performing high risk medical procedures."

The AMA went on to mention that in some states, obstetricians and rural family physicians no longer deliver babies. Meanwhile, high-risk specialists no longer profile trauma care or perform complicated surgical procedures. In discussing medical malpractice, there are two points that we need to consider. The first is that many of the claims brought against doctors and hospitals could well be frivolous. A study of medical malpractice claims was conducted between 2000 and 2004 by the US Department of Justice, Bureau of Justice Statistics. It found that for seven states in the United States, most of the claims were closed without payment. The second point concerns physician's supply. This has continued to outpace population growth. The AMA statistics showed that in 1980, there were 195 physicians for 100,000 people. In 2004, this figure increased to nearly 300 and the argument here is that pressure on the job is not easily acceptable when given as a reason for malpractice.

But what about the insurance that each doctor is required to take out to cover his or her practice? One doctor in the Queens area of New York says that medicine is never about money. It is about treating patients and making sure that they get better. The insurance is extremely high and at the end of the day most doctors try to do a good job without wanting to be millionaires.

Chapter-9

The Homeless

In a city of wealth, hundreds go to bed hungry and a higher number face the problem of homelessness. According to the Coalition for the Homeless, "Each year 100,000 New Yorkers experience homelessness and each night 38,000 homeless persons sleep in a shelter system. This includes more than 16,000 children and 8,000 single adults." In a recent article in New York's *Daily News*, it was stated that New York "is in the midst of a homeless emergency and its only getting worse". What is the cause of homelessness in New York and what can be done to fix it?

The City of New York and more specifically the Bloomberg administration attribute homelessness to the economy. The administration states that homelessness is much worse elsewhere and that its shelter system is not only more humane than it was a decade ago but that it is actually working. But those who advocate for the homeless point to a different picture. They argue that the city has used all sorts of bureaucratic red tape to deprive families from getting welfare or food stamps. What are some of these obstacles?

In 2004, there was a report that the hindrances were endless and there was only one intake center where families could apply for shelter.

This center was located in the Bronx. This meant that people had to get there by bus and subway and this caused a lot of inconvenience. Once the applicant was present, extensive documentation was necessary. These usually include birth certificates, social security numbers, phone numbers, and proof of eviction notices. But even after these documents were presented, there was no guarantee that a family could be given shelter. According to one report, "minor discrepancies may lead to being declared ineligible, forcing the families to return to the intake shelter and begin the process all over again."

Living conditions in the shelters tend to vary but they are generally poor. A study conducted by 'Better Homes Fund' found that homeless children "have twice the health problems of those in homes, including higher rates of asthma, ear infections, stomach problems, and mental health problems." In 2003, a report was published by the US Conference of Mayors that surveyed 25 cities. It found that homelessness and homeless families in New York City was typical of what was taking place in the whole country. Incidentally, New York City did not participate in the study.

Despite this refusal, other statistics show that there was a 26 per cent increase in the request for food in New York, when compared to a 17 per cent increase in 25 other major cities. A figure that was dismal to read was that 51 per cent of those requesting food handouts in New York City were families with children. The Mayor's Conference came to the conclusion that there were three main factors that were responsible for homelessness. They were an increase in unemployment, low wages and salaries and a high cost of living. The conference predicted that in future years, the situation was likely to get worse.

If the situation in 2004 was a crisis, then present day homelessness is nothing short of an emergency that has reached epidemic proportions. In New York City, the housing situation has been studied by a number of agencies with the aim of finding out which neighborhoods have produced the greatest number of homeless families. One of the findings of a "Vera" study shows that nearly half of the homeless families in New York are from 10 community districts.

Another finding was that the previous addresses of most families before they entered a shelter were in the Bronx, Brooklyn or Central Manhattan. A statistical breakdown has revealed that in the Bedford-Stuyvesant area, there were 1,355 homeless residents while East New York had 1,995. Jamaica and Hollis had a population of 913 with Melrose and Morisiana recording the lowest number with 787 persons in homeless shelters.

A worrying statistic is that about 33 per cent of the families who left shelters in 1994 returned within a period of 10 years. There were demographic factors that were responsible for their return. A family that was headed by a single father stood the risk of returning to the shelter, especially if the father was young. There were additional reasons that influenced such a population to return and these had to do with the level of education of the father and his employment status. Another category of returnees was pregnant females and families with a larger number of children. When landlords lose their buildings, large families are forced to look elsewhere for living quarters.

The homeless situation in New York reached a point where one newspaper in 2002 reported that "there are more homeless people in New York City than at any time in the last 20 years." In 2004, Alan

Whyte, a writer on the homeless situation, said that on the night of 2 January 2004, 38,282 homeless people were forced to turn to the city's municipal shelter system. The churches and other private places accounted for another 1,500 beds. What was alarming about this was the fact that at least 16,000 of those who were homeless were children. Today, the average stay for families in a shelter is about 12 months. In 1992, it was about six months.

What is the plan of the City to deal with the growth of homelessness? The Bloomberg administration some years ago set out a plan to move 9,000 families out of the shelter system and place them in apartments. It will be recalled that in Queens, a hotel next to JFK Airport was converted as a residence for the homeless. However, this did not go down well with the local community as it complained of noise pollution and other unacceptable behaviors from the new neighbors.

Moving people into residential homes is a problem for any administration. It is rather surprising that the homeless problem has not surfaced into the 2009 mayoral debates. In September 2002, the Bloomberg administration had plans to move 9,000 families outside of the shelter system. This was seen as a positive long-term solution. But since then the homeless situation has increased. What are the answers? The most obvious is to provide adequate and affordable housing. If this is done, there will be considerable savings to the city. The Independent Budget Office states, "It costs about $36,000 a year for homeless family to stay in a shelter, and about $24,000 a year for a single adult."

A coalition of housing advocates stated in 'Housing First', "The city needs a larger policy to deal with the fundamental issues of housing costs and housing supply which are the root of the crisis." Converting plans into bricks and mortar will help to move away from a policy of temporary placements into a permanent solution. The grant of Section 8 vouchers is seen as a way to move families into subsidized housing. Vouchers are provided to low-income families to help pay rent to landlords who participate in the Section 8 program.

In the 2002 Mayoral Campaign, homelessness was a hot campaign topic. It was one of the much-debated issues of the Bloomberg manifesto. He said at the time that the city needed 100,000 new apartments. Mayor Bloomberg said he would make the case that "we need housing more than we need office space." In the 2009 campaign, education and fiscal management have become the cornerstones but the housing problem has not faded. Bold and imaginative leadership will be needed to stem the rising tide of homelessness.

Chapter-10

Good Manners and Etiquette Wanted

Bad manners will be the death of society. In an old school building in Guyana, set gem-like and fair are three signs that remain as invigorating and fresh as the morning breeze. They read, "Hard work brings its own rewards" and to the left of that is "Quiet speech is a sign of refinement." But perched high on a ceiling is a banner that spans both walls. It is as if the founding fathers of the school wanted to make a special point. The sign painted in red reminded all that "Manners maketh man."

In Guyanese and Caribbean cultures, these sayings were drummed into children daily and woe to those who forgot to say 'please and thank you' or 'good morning or good afternoon' to their elders. The wrath of grandma, that custodian of etiquette, will descend on them with fury for forgetting their 'p's and 'q's. Oh, for the days in which good manners were paramount, where etiquette, decorum and refined speech ruled the day! In the last few years, good manners have taken a beating with the result that to be loud, aggressive and to use profanities galore have become normal behavior.

The fact is that such behavior is far from acceptable and the home, streets and schools have a lot to answer for when it comes to shaping the behavior of the child. Only recently, a 13-year old child in a public school punched a classmate for no reason. When asked by the teacher and guidance counselors to say that he was sorry, the child bluntly refused. Saying sorry, he said, was a sign of weakness. It meant that he was soft. He had to be hard and mean.

This desire to be 'mean' has permeated much of our society with the result that bad attitudes are commonplace. The remarkable lack of civility can be found in even the highest institutions. In recent weeks, there have been three instances of national rudeness that have caught the attention of the public. They have brought to the fore the need for us to take stock and to put manners and etiquette back to where they belong. The first case of national disrespect involved no less than the Presidency itself. President Barack Obama was addressing the Congress on his Health Care Plan when Joe Wilson, a Republican Senator from South Carolina, shouted, "You lie". Democrats insisted that Mr. Wilson had violated the basic rules of decorum and civility. 'You lie' may be a common everyday expression but to accuse the President of doing so when he is addressing the Congress is unthinkable. There is simply no precedent for it.

The 'you lie' statement has drawn the ire of former President Jimmy Carter who has put this down to more than rudeness. According to President Carter, Wilson's outburst was rooted in fears of a black President. "I think it is based on racism," Carter said. "There is an inherent feeling among many in this country that an African-American should not be president," he added. Joe Wilson has since apologized but the damage has been done.

President George Bush, who many felt misled the nation on the

Iraq War, was always treated in public with respect, except for that shoe-throwing incident. It was not the first time that Joe Wilson has found himself at the center of a controversy. In 2003, when Essie Mae Washington-Williams announced that the late Senator Strom Thurmond was her father. Joe Wilson was incensed. He felt that Essie's revelation that she was the bi-racial daughter of Thurmond was a smear on Thurmond's reputation. How can truth be a smear?

Manners are the way in which people interact with each other and politeness is a prized asset. In 2006, the Chief Justice of the Supreme Court in New South Wales, Australia, had quite a mouthful to say about the state of manners in his country. Justice James Spigleman said, "Australian adults and children alike have no manners. Road rage, mobile phone conversations in restaurants, overzealous parents at Saturday sport, noisy ghetto blasters and reality television are just some of the perpetrators of disrespect." Justice Spigleman stated that if children are not taught good manners by the time they go to school, it then becomes difficult to set things straight. Are things any different in the United States?

In a recent survey, more than 50 per cent of Americans are concerned about the growing rudeness in their country. In a poll among mothers, 40 per cent wanted their children to treat adults with respect, while 29 per cent wanted 'please and thank you' to be included in everyday language and 17 per cent wanted their children to learn to share. It is interesting that nearly all the parents wanted their children to say 'sorry' when they have done something wrong. This brings us to the second recent case of disrespect in which the word 'sorry' had to be forced out of someone who should have known better.

Serena Williams is a role model to many young persons. She is athletic, graceful, and has probably the best forehand in tennis. Serena is a champion but her behavior recently was hardly a class act. She was losing to Kim Kligsters at the US Open. In tennis, as in life, there are days when nothing seems to go right. The test is to exercise control and be cool and balanced. The crowds love a winner, but also a gracious loser.

Serena's behavior in which she threatened to do damage to the lineswoman was a violation of the rules of tennis. But more importantly, it spoke volumes about her temperament. What emerged was an ugly, angry and selfish parody of someone trying to rise above herself. After the incident, the guessing game was when would Serena apologize. She too found it difficult to say 'sorry' but after a day of counseling and advice, she released a statement that was contrite and to the point.

The statement said, "I wish to amend my press statement of yesterday, and want to make it as clear as possible. I want to sincerely apologize to the lineswoman, Kim Kligsters, the United States Tennis Association and mostly Tennis fans everywhere for my inappropriate outbursts. I am a woman of great pride, faith and integrity and I admit when I am wrong." She said she would like to lead by example. Another celebrity who should lead by example made a fool of himself by falling prey to bad manners.

Kanye West has it all. He comes from a good family, is talented and has tons of money. You might even think he is simply amazing. But at the 2009 Video Music Awards, Kanye pranced on the stage and in a sublime moment of uncouth manners and boorishness pulled the microphone away from Taylor Swift and said that Beyonce had a better video. The audience was stunned including Beyonce and Taylor Swift. It turns out that this was not a one-off act by Kanye. His other hits extended to 2004. In that year, he lost to country singer Gretchen Wilson. He walked out of the show proclaiming loudly, "I was definitely robbed."

On 2 September 2005, at a fundraising drive for Hurricane Katrina, Kanye ranted on TV that, "George Bush doesn't like black people". Kanye was at it again on 2 November 2006 when he lost the best video award to a French duo at the European Music Awards. He crashed the stage and interrupted their acceptance speech with profanities. In 2007, Kayne said that he was boycotting all future MTV award shows.

What lessons can be drawn from these incidents of bad manners involving these celebrities? The first is that good manners seem to be in short supply with some persons of status. The rich and famous tend to feel that there is a separate standard of behavior for them. When the grudging apologies are made, they are often used to promote the latest book or record or movie. A recent example of supremely bad taste is Joe Jackson, using his son Michael Jackson's death to promote a record company. Joe Wilson, the Senator, is using his new-found fame to hold fundraisers. Serena Williams is plugging her book while Kanye West gets to appear on the 'Leno Show' in primetime.

Bad manners is a national cancer that is eating away at decency and civility. There is urgent need for everyone to begin reinforcing the basics. Manners maketh man… and woman. A National Day of Politeness would be a good starting point.

Chapter-11

Fixing Schools

President Barack Obama has now turned his attention to fixing America's schools. The Presidential Commission Report of 1983 still resonates among educators. The report titled *A Nation at Risk* warned that "the educational foundations of our society are presently being eroded by a rising tide of mediocrity that threatens our very future as a nation and a people." What has changed in the decades that have followed the report? According to some observers, America's schools are still failing us as "they are not preparing enough young people to succeed in the 21st Century workplace."

The statistics in our school system leave room for policies that are urgently needed to fix the problem. In 1989, President George Bush convened a meeting with top education officials to address "the rising tide of mediocrity and to make students in the United States number one in the world in math and sciences". How has the United States fared so far?

The Education Trust in Washington reports that "less than half of America's school children read proficiently at their grade level". Students in the 12th grade in the United States score below teenagers in other developed countries in math and sciences. What is the status of low income and minority students? The statistics for this group show that there is a lot more to be done to boost their academic achievement. Only 29 per cent of fourth graders, for instance, read proficiently at their grade level and among low income children, the number drops to 13 per cent.

The conclusion is that by the end of high school, black and Hispanic children perform below standard at the eighth grade level. There is a growing minority population in the United States, and it is estimated that by 2040, white students will fill "fewer than half of school seats in the United States". Each year, the Bill and Melinda Gates Foundation donates more than 100 million dollars for education reform in the United States. What is worrying for the foundation is that the achievement gap is widening. According to those who are close to the foundation, "the real challenge lies with the continuing mediocrity that plagues too many of America's schools and the disastrous state of education for kids at the bottom."

It is a known fact that each year thousands of children proudly wear their caps and gowns but cannot do math or read proficiently. During George W Bush's time, "No child left behind" became a motto and a political slogan. This suggested that steps would be taken to narrow the achievement gap by improving basic literacy. But more than that, it also reinforced the idea that more students would pass the required state tests and move on to the next level. Why then has "no child left behind" failed to do the trick?

Education is not only about passing tests or spending huge sums of money to build new schools. Education is a sum total of knowledge acquired both from schools and the environment. Ideally, everyone should have an investment in the education of the child, and like a good plant, fruits will not be evident immediately. President Barack Obama has pledged to fix America's schools. He wants to ensure that struggling schools will be helped and good schools will be rewarded.

A few years ago, a number of strategies were outlined to improve the quality of education in the United States. The first relates to teacher quality and commitment. It was found that effective teaching improved math and reading scores. The fact is that many teachers are unqualified in the subject area in which they are teaching. The National Alliance of Business points out that nearly one third of secondary school math and physical education teachers did not major in the subject in which they taught. Teacher quality is also linked to pay. The shortage of quality teachers is related to poor wages, it is argued.

In the present system, many states have uniform salaries for teachers, regardless of their area of specialization. The system does not reward exceptional teachers in reading, math or sciences. There are suggestions to increase teacher pay based on test scores. This is a good suggestion but it does not account for the eighth grader who doesn't know his tables. However, a rewards system for teachers can work as Connecticut has shown. In that state, teacher's salaries have increased and new teachers are asked to pass a test in their subject area. Salaries with continued professional development and student participation can set the stage for reform.

Monetary incentives are a definite fillip to education, especially when they are tied to pay and performance. There is also the argument that schools need to be made smaller, to be broken up into units to make them more manageable. The smaller a school, the more attention can be given to students and staff and the administration will be better able to monitor performance, according to some educators. It is interesting to note that in the 1950s, advocacy groups argued that bigger was better. James B Conant, a former President of Harvard University, was a strong supporter of schools with more than 1,000 students.

In New York City, there are big schools with more than 5,000 students and some have already been broken up, including Jamaica High School, Franklin K Lane and Far Rockaway High School. Today, the argument in favor of smaller schools is that "they're like a village where all the teachers know the students". In recent years, charter schools have increased to offer more variety and greater choice in education. Charter schools are able to circumvent many of the union regulations, thereby making them adaptable to changing conditions. Big schools, on the other hand, are like factories and they show little concern for the individual product, the students, according to some administrators. Learning done in an intimate and personalized environment can work wonders, according to some educators.

What about the role of tests as a means of boosting academic achievement? This is a controversial area that has generated a lot of bitterness. The argument is that students become robotic when they are prepped mainly for tests. But unless there is a major overhaul in the system, tests remain the main yardstick to measure achievement and to determine promotion policies and meet standards. In some states, tests have raised concerns with parents and education boards. In Massachusetts, 45 per cent of high school students fail the tests that were required for college. In Cincinnati, only 35 per cent of students passed all five of the tests that were required for graduation in 2003. There was also a high dropout rate among high school students as a result of test failures. Some educators believe that one way to counter parental criticisms of tests is to "develop tests worth teaching to". However, in states where this has happened and scores have improved, criticisms have still occurred. The object is to strike a happy balance between testing, the completion of the curriculum and the maintenance of high standards. One idea would be to move away from "fill in the bubble" and to request extended answers and analysis based on comprehension.

Section-II

Immigration and Other Issues

Chapter-12

Illegal Immigration Unabated

In the first year of the Obama administration, over 400,000 illegal immigrants were deported. The words of a candidate can flow from the land of milk and honey. The campaign trail becomes a haven where promises are made and where speeches are dramatic and lofty that they can even move statues to tears. But woe to the politician who becomes elected and has to read his campaign promises against the harsh reality of budgetary constraints and difficult committees. During the 2008 Presidential elections, Mr Barack Obama had realized, perhaps more than most, that immigration would be a key factor in some of the swing states. He was also aware of the fact that he was inheriting a broken system and that he needed to take steps to fix it.

Mr Obama had stated that in his first year, he would outline a policy on immigration that would have far-reaching impact. It would be a blueprint for reform. More than a year has passed since Mr Obama took office. It is high time to assess what he has done to fulfill some of these promises. The latest estimate by the United States Customs and Enforcement officials says that undocumented immigrants in the US could be as high as 20 million persons. Under the Bush administration, attempts were made to stem the flow of immigrants into the US.

Bernhard Mueller, a labor attorney in North Carolina, stated that during the Bush administration, "it was more of a big-bang worksite raid, arrest illegal aliens, and hit the news." Worksite raids across America became standard practice and this led to "thousands of undocumented persons being arrested". What has President Obama done differently? Some writers have argued that President Obama has used his executive powers to make changes on immigration, rather than wait for Congress to overhaul the entire system. One major aspect of immigration, as we have seen, concerns worksite raids. In the past, immigration officers would swoop on undocumented workers, but under the Obama administration, the emphasis is now on employers.

According to the *Wall Street Journal*, "Administration officials say they want to shift the emphasis on immigration enforcement to what the White House calls the demand side of illegal immigration by focusing on employers." A senior official in the Obama administration stated that the aim is to target employees who are cheating and who are taking unfair competition out of the market.

Immigration has proven to be a complicated issue long before Mr Obama became President. In the last 20 years, no administration has really come to grips with solving immigration problems. There is the notion that immigration is so complex that it is unsolvable. Under George W Bush, there was a piecemeal approach to immigration with no real attempts to reorganize the status of the millions of undocumented persons living and working in the United States. In the meantime, one hears from the political establishment catch phrases such as 'immigration is the engine' that drives the American economy. If immigration is the engine and is so valued, then one could expect successive administrations to take steps to reform it.

Why is this reluctance to overhaul the system? One of the answers lies in politics. It is no secret that many in Washington have deep suspicions regarding the term ' amnesty'. Republicans on the Hill pointed out that they will not support any measure that includes the word 'amnesty' as this gives the impression that the undocumented are given a free passage to live and work in America. The point is that regardless of terminology, the word 'amnesty' is likely to be used by millions if and when their status is regularized. What is unclear at the moment are the terms and conditions that Mr Obama's policies will take.

There are those who have argued that since he took office, little has changed in Mr Obama's approach to immigration policy. They state that he has made cosmetic niceties that include flowery language but on a practical level people are still harassed and face imprisonment and deportation. The *Washington Post* in May 2009 reported that Homeland Secretary Janet Napolitano has announced only one change from the Bush administration. This concerns the limiting of raids at workplaces. According to the newspaper, more controversial and punitive aspects of Bush's policies are embraced and indeed expanded by Obama.

For example, Obama plans to expand the 1.1 billion dollars program that Bush started, the aim of which would be "to check the immigration status booked into local jails over the next four years.". In addition, "Obama will continue a zero tolerance program that jails any illegal immigrant caught crossing parts of the US-Mexico border. And the administration is admissible of an eight billion dollars virtual fence of tower mounted sensors and cameras along the border." Mr Obama has placed a lot of emphasis on border controls to overhaul the system. He said in April 2009, "If the American people don't feel like you can secure the borders, then it's hard to strike a deal that will get people out of the shadows and on the pathway to citizenship who are already here."

Some advisors who are close to Obama say that Bush's immigration policies were not effective because they were heavy-handed. Has Obama adopted a softer approach toward immigration? Republican Lamar Smith who is a member of the House Judiciary Committee said that a decreased emphasis on deporting non-criminals would amount to a de-facto amnesty for illegal immigrants in the United States. He said that it would also encourage more illegal immigration. One of the worrying aspects of Obama's immigration policy has come, ironically, from Obama himself.

In his State of the Union speech in January 2010, immigration took up a mere sentence in an otherwise bulky address. President Obama said, "And we should continue to work on fixing our broken immigration system to secure our borders, enforce our laws, and ensure that everyone who plays by the rules can contribute to our economy and enrich our nation." Are these few words the real immigration issues that affect our country? Border controls and security are important but what about the millions who live and work in the United States and obey the law? When will the government begin to regularize their status?

Obama's comments on immigration have caused understandable concerns in various immigration reform groups. They feel that he has not given the matter enough attention. For example, thousands of families suffer when deportations occur. The Illinois Coalition for Immigrant and Refugees Rights said that at the current rate, President Obama will deport more than 400,000 immigrants in his first year in office, much more than President Bush did in his first year. The Obama administration then has the responsibility to work quickly to reform immigration and to provide relief to millions who make a vital contribution to the United States.

Chapter-13

New York's Newest Immigrants

The 2008 Phagwah Parade was important in a number of ways. Smiling faces that lined the sidewalk comprised all nationalities. At Smokey Oval Park, it became evident that the Phagwah Parade was reaching out to other nationalities as they sang and danced and helped to usher in Spring in New York. The Phagwah Parade has, after all, been around for 19 years and has become an institution for some of New York's new immigrants. It provides a sense of belonging and identity that is important in any immigrant community. Indo-Caribbeans are only one of the many groups to settle in the United States and bring their culture with them. Every year, people from 87 countries settle in New York City. They number around 110,000 persons. Imagine the number of languages, custom, food, fashion and talent that these countries add to the already rich culture of the city. The statistics are indeed impressive and, in some cases, mind-boggling.

In the 1990s, the top country of origin for immigrants to the United States has been the Dominican Republic with 22,000 a year. Most Dominicans settle in Manhattan or the Bronx, or Washington Heights. When the Soviet Union was dissolved in 1992, the average flow of immigrants from the former republics increased from 1,300 a year to 13,300 a year during 1990–1994. Russian immigrants are to be found in South Brooklyn and in the Brighton Beach area. Jews are also leaving the city of Bukhara in Uzbekistan where over 70 percent of them have settled in Queens, New York.

There is an age factor concerning immigrants to New York. For example, most migrants to New York City are young adults with an average age of 27 years, but for those from the Soviet Union, the median age is 36 years. Dominicans comprise one of the youngest groups where the median is 23 years. The Immigration Act of 1990 has had a profound impact on the numbers entering New York. One of the clauses of the law actually encouraged migration from countries such as Ireland and Poland. Another clause set aside visas for skilled workers and this has boosted immigration from Israel, the Philippines, and China.

The Act meant that many Caribbean countries were at a disadvantage. Jamaica, for instance, sent about 9,000 residents a year in the 1980s to the United States but this was reduced to 6,500 a year in the 1990s. The fifth largest source country is Guyana. Surprisingly, Guyana has been rather consistent as a source country. It sent 6,700 a year in the 1980s and 6,200 a year in the 1990s. But the figure from Guyana has significantly dropped in the last few years due to tight immigration restrictions.

Rudy Giuliani, the former Mayor of New York City, has stated that people leave their countries for New York because they want to do better. This is obvious as it is understandable. Few people leave the shores of an economically depressed area and come to New York not wanting to do better. In migration studies, there is a theory that push and pull factors are responsible for leaving their country and heading for the metropolis. While the push factor cannot be discounted, there is little doubt that the pull of the industrial West is a powerful indicator. This means that the economic motive is perhaps the chief determinant as to whether it is inter or intra-continental migration.

During the years 1995 and 1996, a total of 231,000 immigrants settled in New York. At that time, the New York City Department of Planning stated, "New York continues to draw record numbers of immigrants; numbers not seen since the early decades of the century. The continuing strong influx of human capital into New York City is a key ingredient of our economic strength and the revitalization of our neighborhoods."

It is interesting to note that during this two-year period, the former Soviet Union accounted for 18 per cent of all immigrants to New York City with the Dominican Republic standing at 17 per cent, China with 10 per cent and Jamaica and Guyana at 5 per cent each. It also emerged that the new players were Bangladesh, Egypt, Nigeria and Ghana with significant amounts of new immigrants. What about Mexico? The Mexican population has legally been small, but high rates of fertility and internal migration have led to significant numbers in New York.

In January 2005, the Department of City Planning in New York released its report on New York's newest immigrants. It found that New York's foreign-born population rose from 28 per cent in 1990 to 36 per cent in 2000. The biggest growth occurred in Queens where most migrants settled. Queens and Brooklyn accounted for over two-thirds of the city's immigrants. It is of interest to note that half of the city's residents speak a language other than English at home and about one in four of them has difficulty speaking English.

The 2000 Census has referred to the innovation and dynamism of the new migrants in New York City. One of the main conclusions of the Census is that "the city's demographic future will be shaped by today's immigration patterns: immigrants and their US-born offspring account for 55 per cent of the city's population, and they have made their homes in neighborhoods throughout the city." In addition, 34 per cent under the age of 18 were Hispanic (34 per cent), Blacks non-Hispanic (29 per cent), and Asians (10 per cent). Although first generation immigrants make up 36 per cent of the city's population, they comprise 43 per cent of the labor force. This is ample proof about the extent to which immigrants are helping to reinvigorate the city's economy.

In the summer of 2007, the then Governor Eliot Spitzer had proposed that illegal immigrants be given driving licenses. This became extremely controversial and by November 2007 the plan was abandoned. At that time, a panel was convened to discuss the impact of migrants in New York City. Joseph Berger, a columnist for the *New York Times*, recalled that in the 1950s New York was 'bland'. There were some oddities in the city such as Chinatown. Berger points out that the city has dramatically changed and remade itself.

In 1654, there were 17 languages in New York. In 2008, this has grown to 187 languages. Each language has its own culture attached to it. The practices of their homeland are never far away. Festivals, parades, religion, fashions and foods are integrated and interwoven with those already in New York to form a unique blend that is distinctly cosmopolitan. But the links with their countries of origin do not end there.

Remittances play an important role in cementing bonds between New York and many poor countries. Dominicans in New York remit over a billion dollars to the Dominican Republic every year. Guyanese send 424 million dollars while those from Trinidad remit 124 million dollars. These sums are a vital source of income to many families in developing countries. In some cases, remitted funds are used for development and provides employment for the poor such as in Bangladesh.

As can be seen, today's new immigrants, by their sheer numbers, are different from the old ones. They are busy carving a place for themselves in the big cities, working several jobs to make ends meet. They keep their culture alive by staying close to houses of worship.

Chapter-14

Obama can do Better on Immigration

"We can make a person disappear." This statement was made to a shocked audience at a 2008 Immigration Conference. The speaker was no less than a senior officer of ICE, the immigration service that is part of Homeland Security. In 1995, the Bush administration passed a piece of legislation that continues to be controversial. This law was known as 287(g) and it says that the police "could turn over suspects or criminals to immigration authorities for possible deportation". The police usually do not enforce federal laws. Three years ago, when millions took to the streets to call for immigration reform laws, 287(g) became one of the cornerstone of their protests.

In the 2008 Presidential campaign, Mr Barack Obama promised to work for immigration reforms. Mr Obama went on to say that if he were elected, he would call for comprehensive immigration reforms. Well, two years down the line and we are no closer to a just and fair immigration policy. Everyone agrees that we cannot deport 12 million undocumented persons from the shores of America. We can argue forever as to the terminology that should be used to describe them. It matters little whether it is an "amnesty" or "conditional" pardon or adjustment of status. The fact is that millions of immigrants are making a great contribution to America. They need to come out from the shadows and be given the opportunity to be Americans.

The criticisms that the undocumented immigrants receive on a daily basis would seem to suggest that they are a bunch of criminals who do nothing else but sponge off the American economy. This is not the case at all. Let us look at education. Each year, it is estimated that there are between 50,000 and 70,000 undocumented immigrants who graduate from high schools in the United States. Some of them go on to colleges, facing many hardships in the process.

When these students graduate, it is America that benefits. This is definitely a brain gain for the United States. The point here is that the undocumented are not only filling positions that Americans do not want, but that their children are becoming part of the educated workforce. It is time that the DREAM Act regularizes the status of the children with greater speed. This is something that Lou Dobbs and others would do well to bring to the wider American audience.

Apart from education, the economy in some states will grind to a halt if immigrant labor were absent. President Barack Obama was keenly aware of the importance of immigrant contribution to the United States during the campaign. He actually courted the Hispanic vote in a number of states and had it not been for the Hispanic voting bloc, he could very well have lost the elections. This was on the President's mind when he addressed the Esperanza National Hispanic Breakfast on 19 June 2009.

The President spoke of the promise that America holds out to many of its peoples. He wanted to see a fair immigration policy, to stamp out illegal immigration and to bring to justice employers who exploited undocumented workers. But what about the millions who are already in the United States, have committed no crimes, and want desperately to be officially integrated in the country?

President Obama said, "We must also clarify the status of millions who are here illegally, many who have put down roots. For those who wish to become citizens, we must require them to pay a penalty and pay taxes, learn English, go to the back of the line behind those who play by the rules. That is the fair, practical, and promising way forward and that's what I am committed to passing as President of the United States."

The President went on to say, "We must never forget that time and again, the promise of America has been renewed by immigrants who make their story part of the American story." The President does not need any reminder that hundreds of immigrant soldiers have died in battle to protect the security of the United States.

These fine words were met with great applause but a number of hurdles have presented themselves in the way forward. In the first place, the President's plan has been stymied by the disunity in the House of Representatives. It would appear that for the year 2009, there would be no new immigration law. Secondly, President Obama could change or amend certain aspects of the law that was passed under Bush but he has refused to do so. In fact, he has strengthened some of the old laws to make them even more punitive.

Imagine the scene. A US Citizen is a victim of a crime that was witnessed by an undocumented person. Under the Bush administration, this person would be in real trouble if he or she were to admit witnessing the crime. The person's immigration status would be asked and the police would forward the information to the authorities. The undocumented witness could then be subject to deportation. This sounds like no way to solve crimes since it discourages people from coming forward and helping to apprehend the criminal. This has so incensed human rights groups that they have petitioned the White House with a view of amending the legislation.

In fact, on 1 July 2009, the chiefs of police of 64 urban areas spoke out against 287(g) and the punitive aspects of enforcement against the undocumented. This legislation, as we have seen, compromises the relationship between law enforcement officers and their local communities. What has been the effect of 287(g) on families? According to many observers, the most vulnerable sections of the community have been marginalized. There is also evidence that families have been destroyed and people have been subjected to racial profiling. There is distrust between the police and the community. It is highly unlikely that the undocumented would want to give evidence in criminal cases if their status can be checked and they can be subject to deportation.

What is remarkable is that this piece of legislation can be suspended or amended by the Obama administration. It does not need Senate's approval but how has the Obama administration reacted to criticisms of law 287(g)? In a step that is beyond belief, the administration is actually expanding the 287(g) program. Albert Ruiz, writing in the New York *Daily News* states, "the 287(g) program has been synonymous with racial profiling and human rights abuse. For all its bluster, 287(g)'s main targets have been day laborers and traffic violators. These are the criminal illegal aliens routinely arrested without probable cause, by deputized officers." The Secretary of Homeland Security Janet Napolitano states that she has expanded 287(g) to focus on illegal criminal aliens and not on gardeners but it doesn't sound credible. Sheriff Joe Arpaio of Maricopa County in California runs one of the largest 287(g) programs in the country without oversight.

President Obama met with Mexican President Felipe Calderon and Canada's Prime Minister Stephen Harper and had promised to have an immigration bill ready in 2010. But while the legislation is drafted, the world needs to know more about his policies for those who are stopped at ports of entry. The Obama administration wants to have a civil detention system to replace the current one that oversees 400,000 people who are in custody. One such place, the Hutto Center, has been the subject of much controversy, where facilities are poor and substandard. In addition, the E-Verify system has been described as a step forward and a step back. Janet Napolitano is trying to dissociate the Obama administration from that of the previous administration but it doesn't appear convincing.

Ms Napolitano points out that border security is essential to the welfare of America. One does not doubt this but in her recent speech, not a word was mentioned about the positive impact immigrants are having in America. The Immigration System is broken and unless President Obama radically repairs it, we will have more of the same, despite the flowery language.

Chapter-15

Deportations from America

One in ten American families are of mixed immigration status. A well-rehearsed ritual occurs in the United States twice weekly. At a US military base in Texas, a jet lands to pick up its cargo. On the tarmac are hundreds of men and women in handcuffs and chains. They have been processed and will soon leave the United States for home. Some have spent several years in the US while others may have had shorter stays. On board, the flight is a mixture of laughter and tears and as the plane descends, familiar sights are spotted and there is occasional applause. This plane can land at any airport and the story will be the same. The people who were deported usually vow that in a matter of days, they will try to return to the United States.

The flight on that day was going to Mexico and Ecuador; others will touch Panama, Nicaragua and Colombia. In the coming weeks, those flights may also land in India, Haiti, the Philippines or Guyana. It is estimated that more than 70 per cent of all illegal immigrants in the United States originate from Latin America. A few years ago, when thousands turned up in Manhattan to call for an amnesty, the majority in the crowds were Latinos. Their cries of "*si si puede*" rang loudly in the streets. But Latin America is not the only region that has undocumented people living in the United States. They come from many countries and deportations are occurring at a rapid pace. Some people argue that millions will be deported before an amnesty policy is put into place.

At present, there are about 30,000 Haitians whom the US would like to deport. It is useful to look at the statistics during the period 1996 to 2004 to get an idea of the number of deportations from the US to other countries. As can be expected, Mexico tops the list with 979,172 deportees. This is followed by Honduras with 38,400; Guatemala 37,038; El Salvador 33,062; the Dominican Republic 23,532; Brazil 16,027 and Jamaica with 14,271 respectively. Several countries fall below the 10,000 mark and they are Ecuador with 5,515; Peru 5,449; Haiti 4,433; and the Philippines with 4,305. During that six-year period, deportees of Trinidadian origin totaled 2,251 and those from Guyana were 1,929. According to the figures, in 2004 alone, there were 235,247 persons who were placed in detention by the Bureau of Immigration and Customs Enforcement (ICE).

Once an undocumented person has been detained, he or she is placed in hundreds of local prisons throughout the United States, some of which are privately contracted. A person can be deported for over-staying his or her visa or by committing a felony. Deportation can also occur even though an individual may have a green card. If a person is found guilty of an offence while in possession of a green card, then that person is also subject to deportation. Most of what is classified as 'offence' fall under the 1996 laws. Those laws strengthened the grounds of inadmissibility to the United States. They were reinforced after 11 September 2001 when the Department of Homeland Security deported thousands of persons of Middle Eastern origin.

Persons who are rounded up for deportation are subject to arbitrary punishment that can include solitary confinement, the lack of basic medical needs, regular outdoor exercise and even sexual abuse. The effect on families is often devastating. Deportation causes thousands of children who are born in America to lose their mom or dad. Senator Ted Kennedy has harsh words for the 1996 immigration laws and their impact on families. According to him, "The laws have had harsh consequences that punished families and violated individual liberty, fairness and due process. Families are being torn apart. Persons who present no danger to their communities have been left to languish in INS detention."

Nancy Pelosi, Harry Reid, and others state that they are "opposed to mandatory and indefinite detention of immigrants and support adherence to guidelines that assure appropriate conditions of detention, including access to legal counsel". While the elected representatives were asking for fairness and due process, New Jersey reported that it had actually stepped up its removal of undocumented immigrants. For example, the *Star Ledger* stated in November 2008 that the number of immigrants seized in New Jersey and deported to their native country jumped by 25 per cent from 3,339 in 2007 to 4,194 in 2008.

There are two important factors that are connected to immigration policy in the short term. The first is that of cost or economics while the second relates to crime and the deportee. The number of undocumented persons in the United States is estimated to be between 12 and 38 million persons. Is it realistic to deport them all to their native countries? According to Shai Goldstein of the New Jersey

Immigration Policy Network, "It is impossible to deport 12 million people without spending trillions of dollars. It is not cost effective. It's bad public policy. We need to have an federal immigration policy that is fair, humanitarian and grounded in reality."

There are around 560,000 persons who have committed offences in the US and are running from the law. Mexico was home to 77 per cent of the criminals who were deported in 2005 but there were other countries on the list as well. In February 2009, a group of 65 Nigerians were deported for various offences and a similar number of Filipinos were also deported. Apart from New Jersey, the state of Florida has seen an increase of deportees. In 2003, Florida deported 7,695 persons, but in the first six months of 2008, it had deported 6,000 persons. The home countries were Colombia, Guyana, Haiti, Jamaica and Mexico.

The second factor concerns criminals who are deported, set up cells and gangs at home, and revert to crime in a short space of time. The impact of deportees on the crime situation in their own countries is not fully understood, although there is a link between deportation and local criminal activity. In one case study in El Salvador, the results were inconclusive. President Barack Obama has stated that he intends to restart the immigration debate with a view to regularize the status of many of those who are undocumented. This is welcome news and the Summit of the Americas in Trinidad should place immigration on top of its agenda.

Recently, a group of Latin American leaders met with Vice President Joe Biden and asked for deportations from America to be slowed. It was evident that economics was on their minds. For example, deportations have hit Latin America hard. In the last quarter of 2008, remittances to Latin America from the US fell by four per cent, according to the Inter-American Development Bank. Clearly, a comprehensive immigration policy needs to be put in place and one can only hope that this year will see the start of those talks.

Chapter-16

Detention in America

When Francisco Castaneda felt a pain in his penis, he was understandably worried. But he thought he was in good hands. He was in a facility where doctors and other personnel could help. Castaneda was hardly a law-abiding citizen. In fact, he was an illegal immigrant who had a drug conviction. He was born in El Salvador and came to the United States when he was 10 years old. As a result of his conviction and immigration status, Castaneda was picked up by immigration officers and taken to a detention center in San Diego, California. This happened on 26 March 2007. It was the following day that he informed the doctors of the pain in his genitals.

Castaneda was seen by a physician's assistant who recommended that he saw a urologist so that a biopsy could be arranged. This was to assess the possibility of cancer cells present. Time passed and nothing happened. The situation worsened for Castaneda. He filed grievances with the Department of Immigration and Health Services (DIHS). In one of those grievances, he wrote, "I am in considerable amount of pain and I am in desperate need of medical attention." The Department replied that the surgery was elective and wouldn't pay for it. Castaneda's request was denied for nearly a year. Then the unthinkable happened.

One day in February 2007, the immigration authorities went to see him. They told him he was free to leave. Just like that! Castaneda who was detained for breaking immigration laws and had a drug conviction was now free to go without any penalty and without any explanation given by the immigration department! On 8 February 2007, Castaneda had his biopsy. He was diagnosed with cancer. His penis was amputated six days later. Unfortunately, the cancer had already spread and Francisco Castaneda died a year later.

Los Angeles Federal Judge, Dean Pregerson, in his ruling castigated the actions of the US Immigration Department. The judge further indicated that the actions of the Immigration Customs Enforcement (ICE) "bespeaks of conduct that transcends negligence by miles". What was the lesson of the Castaneda case? It was one of negligence and a total disregard for the suffering of others. But the motive appears to be that since a person is detained in a detention facility, he or she is open to abuse. If you think that Fransisco Castaneda's case is singular, you are mistaken.

Reverend Joseph Dantica, an 81 year-old respected Haitian was confronted by hoodlums in his country. They threatened violence against him. One relative recounted what precipitated Rev Dantica to leave Haiti. She said, "When the combined Haitian and international forces left Bel-Air, gang members came to my uncle's home, told him 15 of his friends had been killed and said that he had to pay for the burials or die." Rev Dantica grabbed a few papers and fled the country for America. He had multiple entry visas for the US in his passport. When he arrived at Miami International Airport, he was arrested. Three days later, in obvious discomfort and pain, he suffered from convulsions and died. His niece, the Haitian prize-winning author Edwige Dantica, in an Op-ed in the *New York Times* wrote, "Like the claims from Cubans, Haitian asylum claims should be considered humanely and fairly so that calamities like my uncle's flight and eventual death in the custody of the Homeland Security Department are never repeated."

The fact is that Rev Dantica was one of many detainees in the 22 detention centers in the United States. In the case of Rev Dantica, the physician at the detention center in Miami said that he died from pancreatitis. It took him four hours to get Rev Dantica to an outside hospital. When confronted by Edwige Dantica, the doctor said that the Reverend was "faking it". The Statue of Liberty has the famous inscription about wanting the "huddled masses yearning to breathe free". But things have changed, and not for the better, especially for those who are detained in America. In 2007, Juan Guevara was placed in detention. He began to complain of severe headaches. It was not long after that he died of brain aneurysm. According to a staff member, "The detainee was prescribed Tylenol. He was not seen or evaluated by an RN, mid-level physician's assistant or a physician." The department's own reviews stated that there is critical staffing shortages, a 48 per cent nursing vacancy rate. While the number of immigrants in detention has tripled since 11 September 2001, the health services budget has grown by only 65 per cent.

The case of another immigrant who was detained in 2007 presents a shocking example of a system that is broken. Somalia is a country that is ruled by clans and warlords. There is no rule of law and violence is the order of the day. Amina Mudey grew up surrounded by this violence. Her father, brother and sisters were murdered in Somalia. Numbed by the violence and wanting to escape further atrocities, Amina traveled to the United States and sought political asylum. She appeared to have a compelling case but not in the eyes of the Immigration Department.

Amina was placed in shackles after she landed at the airport and taken to a detention center in New Jersey. She was in obvious trauma after a harrowing trip. Counseling, therapy and kindness were replaced by detention and the prescription of a powerful anti-psychotic drug Risperdal. Why was this drug prescribed? The Immigration Department argued that when Amina was taken into the center, she appeared disoriented. Lacking a proper psychological evaluation, the center concluded that Amina needed a powerful drug to keep her in check.

Dazed and at times incoherent, Amina was represented by a human rights group who provided her with doctors. She was taken off the drug and was able to function normally. She was granted political asylum and is now studying computer technology. The cases highlighted so far bring into question a number of issues. First, in the face of negative publicity, the Immigration and Custom Enforcement has decided to tell its own side of the story. In a series of publications, the agency said that the perception of cruelty was misleading.

In discussing detainee health care, ICE stated that the programs on CBS television and the *New York Times* reports were misleading and inflammatory. They provided statistics to show that in 2005, the mortality rates for detainees was 7.5 per cent per 100,000 cases and that their new oversight procedures had helped to decrease mortality even further to 4.3 per cent in 2007. The Immigration Center criticized the media for failing to mention the improvements and concluded that immigration employees are 'trained to spot suicide risks and to use prevention and intervention techniques'.

The department did not respond directly to the cases of Castaneda, Dantica, Amina, and the others. However, it did raise an important point regarding illegal immigrants when it stated that "the detention of individuals who are unlawfully present in the United States and pending removal raises strong opinions and merits a more balanced view."

In other words, should the United States give first-rate medical care to people who are breaking the law and at the taxpayer's expense? This is a question that will always be asked when immigration and detention is discussed. The most appropriate answer comes from Attorney Conan Doyle who represented Francisco Castaneda. Doyle is adamant that "the Supreme Court has said that they are entitled to reasonable medical care, and that includes medical care for any serious medical need." In addition, he points out that America has broken the law and every civilized society should be judged by the way it treats its prisoners. If this is so, then the United States certainly has a long way to go.

Section-III

Health and Drugs

Chapter-17

Bottled Water is From the Tap

A week ago, the world of water cascaded into a sea of foamy bitterness. But the model on television carried on with her smile anyway. She pirouetted with a bottle and drank it with relish. The message was clear. The bottled water was fresh from a mountain glen, where springs run eternal and where nature is captured in all its untainted glory. Every hour, thousands of health-conscious devotees fall for the message on the bottle. The sale of bottled water in 2006 amounted to 12 billion dollars and increases every year. As giant corporations compete for the wallets of consumers, imagine the shock that came with the latest revelations.

A recent report in New York's *Daily News* stated that one of its premier line of water, 'Acquafina', which is bottled by Pepsi, comes from a tap in your kitchen sink. For years, there have been suspicions that the average consumer is being duped and misled by the glossy labels on bottles and packages. Now the water with the "pure, perfect taste" has agreed to insert on the label the acronym 'p.w.s' which stands for 'public water source'. Michelle Naughton, spokeswoman for Pepsi, is quoted as saying that if Acquafina's new label "helps clarify the fact that the water originates from public sources, then it's a reasonable thing to do".

This change of policy by Pepsi took years of work by various groups that are concerned with public accountability. Pepsi, to its credit, has bowed to public pressure and this may endear it to the consumers. However, Coca Cola, another giant corporation, has made no such admission about Dasani water. A number of reports have concluded that Dasani water is also from the tap. The spokes-woman from Coca Cola, Dina Ciardanta, was diplomatic. She said, "We don't believe that consumers are confused about the source of Dasani water." What does this really mean?

These 'tapped confessions' have played straight into the hands of New York's Mayor, Michael Bloomberg. The Mayor, staying clear of the corporate controversy, is urging New Yorkers to drink tap water instead of the bottled variety. He said that "tap water is healthy, delicious, is easier on the wallet and on the environment." There are now steps to replace water coolers with tap water in city departments.

Corporate accountability does not apply to water in bottles only. According to officials in the food industry, the food served in schools may include growth hormones or may be harvested from genetically engineered crops. When mass scale big-business agriculture rely heavily on pesticides, genetic engineering is possible and humans become the guinea pigs.

For the first time in history, mankind is faced with an epic dilemma. There are now an equal number of people (1.1 billion) who get too much to eat as those who do not have enough to eat. This situation presents two sides of a global food epidemic. They are hunger and obesity. Big agribusiness has presented itself as the solution to world hunger, but in 2003 just 8 per cent of American farms accounted for 72 per cent of sales.

In 2005, the water policy of Coca Cola was challenged. It was pointed out that Coca Cola drains the water supplies to sell bottled water and soft drinks. In essence, it monopolizes water. For example, in India the bottling facilities have had a devastating impact on local communities that five Indian communities face water shortages and health problems. It is alleged that Coca Cola uses political influence to get away with irresponsible behavior. At a recent shareholders meeting of Coca Cola, there were protests about the abuses of the corporation.

Tony Clarke, Director of Polaris Institute, has stated recently, "Coke promoted Dasani as safer and healthier than tap water. Prove it." Gigi Kellett of Corporate Accountability has also said that "to add insult to injury, leading brands like Coke's Dasani and Pepsi's Aquafina use tap water as their source." In response to this article, Pepsi has released a statement refuting the latest reports. The release states that Aquafina is not tap water; it is purified drinking water that has gone through several stages to be wholesome.

The bottle water corporations are not the only ones facing public scrutiny and accountability problems. In a recent on-line poll to determine "a corporate Hall of Shame" over 8,000 persons responded. The top three inductees were: ExxonMobil, Halliburton and WalMart. ExxonMobil is the most profitable corporation in the world but the oil giant is using every legal trick in the book to avoid paying five billion dollars that occurred from the Exxon Valdez oil spill that occurred in 1989. It is claimed that ExxonMobil is also stalling action on global warming. It has spent to date nearly 16 million dollars to oppose action on global warming.

Halliburton continues to make big profits from the Iraq war. Since the start of the war Halliburton has been awarded over 20 billion dollars in contracts. Congress is currently investigating three billion dollars in waste and overcharging, including bills for three times the meals that US troops actually ate in Iraq. Halliburton has moved its headquarters from Houston to Dubai. Is this done to pay less US taxes? Then there is WalMart, the largest retail complex in the world.

According to statistics, 2.5 cents of every dollar spent in the US passes through a WalMart cash register. The employees, however, do not benefit from a profit sharing policy. Most of them have an income that is on par with the poverty level. WalMart was recently taken to court in the largest sex discrimination suit on record. It involves over one million women. The comments about WalMart practices range from its 'predatory merchandising using foreign labor' to 'WalMart is a symbol of what is wrong in America'. It is interesting to note that WalMart has not received a license to operate in New York City, despite repeated attempts.

Corporate accountability is at the heart of a healthy life. Only a few days ago, a consumer report stated that children and adults could be getting more caffeine than is necessary. Most adults can consume up to 400 milligrams of caffeine a day without side effects. Children should have no more than 100 mg per day but new energy drinks such as Celsius has up to 200 mg in a 12-ounce bottle. There are no official US guidelines on caffeine and manufacturers are getting away with this loophole.

In early August, Americans woke up to the news concerning the collapse of a bridge in Minneapolis. This tragedy took several lives. Since the collapse, it is difficult to pinpoint who is responsible. The amount of finger-pointing has been simply astounding. The message for the average consumer is that public corporations can charm the birds off the trees to sell their products. However, when it comes to accepting responsibility for negligence, their statements are usually couched in legalese that ordinary consumers find difficult to understand. Checking the fine print and holding corporations responsible for their slogans are good ways to agitate against corporate greed.

Chapter-18

Obama's Health Plan

There are 50 million Americans who are uninsured. A few years ago, an American lady fell sick in Central London. She was pregnant and as a precaution she was rushed to University College Hospital in London. After an unfortunate series of complications, her baby was delivered without reaching full term. The woman was confined to the hospital for six weeks. During that time, there was a battery of services that was provided for her and the baby. When it came time for her to leave the hospital, these services were also made available and they included counseling, therapy and information on baby care. No mention was made of insurance or money. The objective was to ensure that mother and child were doing well. Once this was done, the lady was presented with a bill for 10,000 pounds that is equivalent to about 20,000 dollars.

The treatment that was provided to our American visitor would cost hundreds of thousands of dollars in the United States. In a lot of cases, this would be beyond the budget of many families. In Britain, the National Health Service (NHS) has been a model for the rest of the world. The NHS is a contract with the British public. It is publicly owned. Hospitals and ancillary services are funded through taxation.

Doctors and nurses receive their salaries under terms and conditions that are agreed upon nationally.

The example of Britain has been cited to show that despite its imperfections, the NHS is perceived by many as a system that works. The NHS was created in 1948 by a 'socialist' Labor Government but the founding fathers did not rule out choice. There is the private sector to supply care for those who can pay and who want to avoid waiting. In the United States where no NHS exists, the uninsured are often left to fend for themselves. The dictum seems to say that "if you are poor or uninsured, try not to get sick".

Some experts, including Cutler, argue that insurers "make money by dumping sick patients and not by keeping people healthy". Preventive services are lacking as well. It is estimated that "in today's health care market, less than 1 dollar in 25 goes for prevention, even though preventive services are among the most cost effective medical services around." President Barack Obama in his Health Care Plan wants to establish a contract with the people. He wants to expand coverage and bring down costs. Mr Obama has outlined a series of principles that he hopes will address the health-care needs of America.

What are these principles? Mr Obama would like to use more technology to access health records. He supports the idea of having more research on illnesses ranging from hypertension to HIV/AIDS. Another proposal is to recruit and train more professionals such as doctors, dentists and nurses and to expand childcare. Mr Obama wants to create 'nurse home visits' for first time mothers. Remember our American mother in London who had access to this facility? The Health Care Bill seeks to strengthen the efficiency of Medicare and to increase food safety by investing billions for Food and Drug Administration Inspections.

The research that was done on American health care and published only recently pointed out that by 2012 affordable coverage is possible as long as plans are put in place by 2010. The estimated cost is set at three billion dollars. The Commonwealth Fund, which sponsored the research, proposes a choice of affordable and accessible private plans, and a new public plan that also cost less to administer.

The health care portion of the Obama budget stipulate that 634 billion dollars will help pay for health care reform over the next 10 years of which 318 billion will come from tax increases. Wealthy seniors will have to pay for more Medicare Part D while cutting Medicare HMO payments by 175 billion is on the agenda. The Plan expects that "the biggest spending reduction is the cut to Medicare HMO payments. This one is hardly a risky political move as everyone has expected it."

The Obama Health Plan has been the subject of many criticisms. Is the Obama Plan a bargain? The first major concern is that Obama is promising the world in terms of health care but how is he going to pay for it? The only way he can heavily subsidize premiums is to raise taxes. It is argued that it is the middle class that would have to pay for it. The plan will cost more than 200 billion a year by 2019. Then there are interpretations by the state and federal governments on the laws. For example, the state would establish insurance exchange while the federal government would improve minimum standards that are more expensive. It is not clear how both will work.

The main problem with the Obama Plan is that costs would

increase and these would be passed on to the consumer. How, for example, would the public option work? According to Tully, who writes on health issues, under the public option, "the exchanges would offer a plan resembling Medicare for more than 100 million Americans. Today, most of them are covered by their employer's plans. But the Democrats' proposals contain a 'pay or play' provision that would allow companies in effect to drop their coverage and substitute a payroll tax."

Economists argue that the public plan will be heavily subsidized and Americans may very well consume more services than are necessary. A bigger number of patients mean soaring costs and physicians may not be able to cope with the demand. When the lines become long, the government will have to spend more to meet the demand. Where will the money come from? It will have to be generated from taxes and some observers feel that it is the middle classes who will feel the pinch.

During the Town Hall meetings, the Democrats have tried to make it clear that the public option means that people can keep their plans and that the private sector cannot refuse those without plans who may need treatment. Would private insurance companies really honor this contract? Public opinion seems to be doubtful about this approach. Paul Krugman, writing in the *New York Times* states, "It's hard to avoid the sense that Mr Obama has wasted months trying to appease people who can't be appeased, and who take every concession as a sign that he can be rolled."

President Obama is brave to tackle a complicated issue such as health care but he must if millions of Americans are to have access to care. It will require intensive work and not everyone will be pleased, but we cannot live in a society in which a sizeable proportion of America is worse off than many Third World republics. The bottom line is that the elephant in the room is the patient. Health campaigns should aim at lifestyle changes while progressive attempts should be made to explore a role for alternative medicine in the conventional setting.

Chapter-19

The Great Vytorin Debate

We live in a society of bills and pills. Ms Mary Jones anxiously awaited the result of her "blood work". She was suffering from high blood pressure and diabetes and her doctor suspected that her cholesterol might be high as well. Her blood test confirmed that her LDL (Low-density lipoprotein) or bad cholesterol was indeed high. She was prescribed Vytorin, a popular anti-cholesterol drug and was told to take a pill every night before going to bed. This was in addition to her medication for high blood pressure and diabetes. Ms Jones took a bunch of pills every night and her co-payment, with her insurance plan, amounted to $70 per month. She was poor but she needed the pills to stay alive.

You can imagine Ms Jones' surprise when she heard the news that one of the pills she was taking can cause cancer. Vytorin is at the center of a furious debate as to its potency as a cholesterol-reducing drug. The manufacturers stand to lose billions of dollars if people refuse to buy Vytorin. The drug industry is a billion dollar enterprise and no manufacturer wants to lose lucrative contracts. But do they really care if you are sick, if their medicines work, or if you become crazy, or even die from their drugs?

The reality is that some medicines can make a person sicker than he or she was at any given time. Take the case of Risperdal, the anti-psychotic drug. In May 2007, the *New York Times* reported that doctors had prescribed the drug for eating disorders and that the side effects in children were harmful. What was alarming was the relationship between the doctors and the drug companies in the promotion of particular brands of drugs, including Risperdal.

According to the *New York Times*, "The intersection of money and medicine, and its effect on the well being of patients has become one of the most contentious issues in health care. Nowhere is that more true than in psychiatry, where increasing payments to doctors have coincided with the growing use in children of a relatively new class of drugs known as atypical anti-psychotics." The newspaper went on to state that "doctors are free to prescribe as they see fit, and drug companies can sidestep marketing prohibitions by paying doctors to give lectures, in which, if asked, they may discuss unapproved uses."

In layman's terms, drug companies and doctors work in collusion with each other. Doctors help market products and have a vested interest in the widespread use of a drug. Vytorin makes billions of dollars for its manufacturers. The drug companies flood the market with it and doctors widely prescribe it. The pie is shared and everyone is happy, except the patient. But the supporters of Vytorin, mainly the manufacturers and some doctors, have defended the use of the medication.

Merch and Schering-Plough jointly make Vytorin and Zetia. They say that ezetimibe, the generic name for Zetia, showed no cancer risk in animals and that "the cancer risk in animal trials is minimal and argued that the cancer finding is as a result of chance." In January 2008, after two years of waiting for the results, the clinical trials involving Vytorin were released. It showed that while the LDL or bad cholesterol was reduced, the drug had little effect on the buildup of plaque in the arteries.

It is this buildup that can lead to a heart attack or stroke. This finding prompted Dr Steven Nissen, the chairman of cardiovascular medicine at the Cleveland Clinic, to say, "This study shows that it matters how you lower cholesterol not just how much you lower cholesterol." The conclusion by Dr Nissen was that "we just don't know what Vytorin does, because we don't have the clinical trials. We know Vytorin blocks absorption of cholesterol but what else does it block in something else in the diet that could be beneficial? We just don't understand fully how it works."

Vytorin is the combination of two drugs, simvastatin that is known as Zucor and ezetimibe made by Shering-Plough. In a response to Dr Nissen's comments, Lee Davies, a spokesperson for Shering-Plough, told *Time* magazine that a conclusive opinion on the use of Vytorin was difficult to get. He blamed the time it took to read and interpret tens of thousands of carotid arteries that the study generated. However, it was pointed out that three larger studies were undertaken and their results would be out by 2012. Will they show anything different? We have to wait for the results.

As the medical world and millions of Vytorin users awaited with fluttering hearts, the debate raged. In April 2008 at a meeting of the American College of Cardiology, Dr Harlan Krumholz from Yale University was quite clear about the use of Vytorin. Dr Krumholz was head of a four-doctor panel that met to review the enhanced trial of the drug. Dr Krumholz recommended that Vytorin should not be used as a first or second line therapy drug. He stated further that, "we have little data about Vytorin and what we have does not inspire confidence."

In early September 2008, the *New York Times* on its front page stated that only a small number of clinical trials were done on Vytorin. However, extensive advertising has made Vytorin one of the best-selling drugs in the world. More than three million people take it every day with sales reaching $5 billion last year. Scientists are now debating whether there is a link between Vytorin and cancer.

According to a report in August 2008, scientists have said that patients "in three clinical trials had a 40 per cent higher chance of dying of cancer if they took Vytorin instead of a sugar pill or another medicine." Dr Allen J Taylor of the Walter Reid Army Medical Center is against the selling of the drug. He believes that the only place people should be taking Vytorin is in a clinical trial. In the latest development, researchers have stated that the drug should be used with caution until more is known.

The New England Journal of Medicine published results online from one study and did an analysis of partial results from two others. Dr Christer Hoglund, a cardiologist at Sweden's Karolinska Institute, summed up the controversy about Vytorin by saying, "We don't know that the drug is bad, but we don't know that it's any good either." In view of this uncertainty, those who are on Vytorin should seriously consider other options.

Chapter-20

Drugs in Sports

The Greeks ate the testicles of a ram to boost their athletic performance. That was in the 8th Century BC. Twelve hundred years later, America experienced a combustible moment. Barry Bonds of the San Francisco Giants broke Hank Aaron's record of home runs. However, the celebrations were diluted with discussions of performance-enhancing drugs, including steroids. In the year 490 BC, the Persians landed at Marathon, 25 miles from Athens. Fearing that the Persians would overtake them, the Athenians sent a message for Pheidippides to run to Sparta to get help. Pheidippides ran 150 miles in two days. The Spartans were late. Although the Athenians were outnumbered 5-1, they defeated the Persians. Pheidippides was sent to run back to Athens to report victory.

When he arrived, he managed to scream "we won" before dropping dead from exhaustion. In 1896, the marathon was run in the first modern Olympic games. It has become ideal for athletes who give their hearts for their country, inspired by the heroism and legend of Pheidippides.

In sports today, the joy, passion and glory are tainted by match-fixing and sleight of hand practices. However, the cancer that is eating away at the integrity of sport is doping or drug taking by athletes. Feats that should be greeted with revelry are tainted and cause anxiety among sport lovers. Deep within the story of a man conquering his Everest lie the residue of the tiny grandmother hurling Forever Mountain in the distance, untouched by scandals. It appears that accusations of drug-taking will always dog the career of Barry Bonds.

The specter of performance-enhancing drugs has become an integral part of sport. In the 1904 Olympics, Thomas Hicks was found to have brandy mixed with strychnine during the marathon. In the 1988 Olympics, Ben Johnson, the Canadian sprinter, ran the 100 meters to sublime perfection. As the world celebrated his world record, Johnson was asked to take a drug test. It turned out that Johnson had taken steroid as well as Dianabol, Furazabol, Cypionate, and human growth hormones. He was stripped of his medal and left the Olympic in disgrace. Carl Lewis was awarded the gold medal instead.

Drugs in sport have become quite fashionable despite the efforts of sports administration to curb their use. Many athletes feel that they can "beat the test" and so continue to use them regardless of consequences. A recent NCAA study shows that marijuana use among student athletes has increased in the last four years. Substances that are prohibited by most sporting committees are stimulants, anabolic agents, diuretics and peptide hormones.

These substances have different effects on the human body. They can increase alertness by reducing fatigue and give the athlete a competitive edge. One of the most popular drugs used by athletes is anabolic steroids. In his State of the Union address, President George W Bush had called on athletes to end the use of steroids.

According to the National Institute of Drug Abuse, the non-medical use of steroid has increased steadily since 1996. For example, it rose from two per cent in 1996 among 12 graders to four per cent in 2002. This increase does not fare well for our youth. The side effects can include liver tumors, cancer, jaundice, high blood pressure, severe acne, and trembling.

How prevalent is the use of drugs in modern day sports? In recent times, some of the most prominent athletes have been linked to drugs. Mary Ann Jones who ran brilliantly for the US in track and field has seen her name linked to performance-enhancing drugs. The same applies to Floyd Landis who has been fighting to salvage his reputation in the Tour de France. In 1998, the entire Festina team in the Tour de France left in shame after various drugs were found in their car. In 2006, Spanish police arrested a sporting director for running a doping ring. As can be seen, the list is extensive and athletes in nearly every sport have been associated with drugs. But it is in baseball that the strongest proof and disdain for drugs has emerged. John Rocker and David Bell have been mentioned as knowing a great deal about 'applied pharmacy'. Accusations about baseball and drugs are so rife that it led Bud Selig, the Commissioner, to begin a full-scale investigation into the use of performance-enhancing drugs. On 3 March 2006, the Senate majority leader George Mitchell was selected to head an open-ended investigation.

The top baseball players immediately refused to co-operate, calling the investigation a 'witch hunt'. It was Jose Canseco in his biography *Juiced* who spilled the beans on his fellow players. The names he identified rocked baseball to its core. In May 2002, Canseco became the first player to admit publicly that he used steroids during his professional career. His book led to a congressional hearing. There were testimony from other greats such as Mark McGwire, Sammy Sosa, Kurt Schilling and others. Canseco claimed in his book that he had to educate many players on how to use drugs properly.

Canseco justified the use of steroids and financial grounds. He claimed that a player couldn't be blamed if steroids meant the difference between making a million dollars and not being able to feed his family. In 1997, when President Bill Clinton was busy explaining about "that woman" Monica Lewinsky, attention was diverted by the exploits of Mark McGwire. He had a 29 million dollar extension with the Cardinals at the end of the 1997 season. When McGwire was healthy, he hit 52 home runs in 1996 and 58 in 1997.

But Canseco claimed to shape part of the McGwire legend. He reported that he personally injected McGwire with steroids. Canseco describes himself as a 'steroid guru' promoting the use of steroids to help prolong the fountain of youth. These days, it is difficult to know who is on drugs when they compete. But one thing is clear. Eventually, the athlete's indiscretions will be brought to light, and when this happens, years of hard work and adulation will fall to pieces. It is much better to play by the rules and stay pure in body and mind.

Drugs in the Olympics

Caesar Augustus banned the Olympics when he conquered Greece. It took a while for modern Olympics to be revived, but in interim, drugs and other substances were used with telling effect. In ancient Greece, mushrooms and plant seeds were ground and ingested to boost the energy of athletes. In Caesar's Rome, the chariot racers used a combination of herbs to build stamina and even their horses were fed special grains. Over the years, athletes have experimented with various substances to gain advantage over their opponents. The results have left bitterness and ire far beyond the sporting stadiums.

In 1886, cyclist Arthor Linton died from an overdose of trimethyl. This drug is linked to the growth of cells in the body. In 1904, another tragedy took place when marathon runner Thomas Hicks collapsed after taking brandy mixed with strychnine. In the two decades, 1930 to 1950, drugs began to alter the complexion of sports. The Olympic games became the main arena for drug-taking. Amphetamines were produced in massive quantities and by the end of the 50s, the Soviet Union and America were competing with each other to produce illegal drugs.

The Soviet Union produced male hormones and America responded with steroids. At the Rome Olympics in 1960, a Danish cyclist died from an amphetamine overdose. However, it was not until 1968 in the Mexico City that the International Olympic Committee (IOC) began to carry out testing for banned substances. Four years later, the Olympic games were caught up in another drug scandal as Dr Bjorn Ekhlom invented a blood packing system to increase the concentration of red blood cells.

At the 1996 Games, East German swimmers won 11 out 13 events and it wasn't until 20 years later that it was discovered that those swimmers were pumped up with steroids. Who can forget the 1988 Games in Seoul, South Korea? Ben Johnson, representing Canada, won his heats and made it to the 100-meter finals. He was running alongside Carl Lewis of the United States. The race had everything, including drama and drugs. Johnson and Lewis took off like two jet planes, and nine seconds and a bit later, it was Johnson who breasted the tape with a world record win.

The celebration was wild, especially in Canada. But the high fives were short lived. Ben Johnson failed a routine drug test, was stripped of his gold medal and banished into ignominy. His gold medal incidentally went to Carl Lewis. Ben Johnson was perhaps the highest profile case at the time. Many thought that this would prove to be a deterrent but this was not the case at all.

In 1994, the Argentine footballer Diego Maradona was banned from the World Cup for "taking a cocktail of five drugs". Two years later, Michelle Smith from Ireland won four swimming gold medals at the Atlanta Games. In 1998, she was found guilty of manipulating drug samples and was banned from competition for four years.

The year 1998 proved to be a momentous one for drugs and sport. In that year, the Festina Team was expelled from the Tour de France after trainer Willy Voet was caught with 400 vials of steroids. Before the year was out, American gold medalist, Florence Griffith-Joyner died of a heart seizure. Was her death as a result of drugs? The Tour de France scandal was so severe that in 1999, the World Anti-Doping Agency (WADA) was established. This proved ineffective and a few months later the Nandrolone controversy broke out. Many athletes including Linford Christie, Petr Korda and Dougie Walker were implicated.

One of the biggest blows to sports came in 2000 when Manfred

Ewald, former president of the East German Olympic Committee, went on trial. He was charged with being an accessory to causing bodily harm. Alain Baxter, who skied for Britain, was stripped of his Bronze medal for using an inhaler and British sprinter Dwain Chambers tested positive for anabolic steroids. This was in 2003 and in the following year, Greg Rusedski tested positive for nandrolone.

These many examples have shown the extent to which drugs have infiltrated sport. For the 2008 games in Beijing, the IOC had on its agenda an item to discuss whether to allow the Greek athlete Katarine Thanou to compete or not. Her drug problem stemmed from the Olympics in Athens when she failed to report for a drug test. She was banned for two years after missing the third drug test.

The Greek team had included her for Beijing. Had she been banned from the Beijing Games as well, she said that she would have sued the IOC President, Jacques Rogge. In the meantime, the IOC had already banned 17 athletes who had tested positive for drugs. According to Rogge, "This is as a result of a deliberate strategy and policy. There were 17 cheats who will not falsify the competition in Beijing."

Despite the actions of Rogge and the IOC, the most chilling warning for Beijing had come from Victor Conte. He was a musician who became a businessman and who many believe is responsible for the BALCO scandal. As far as drugs and the Olympics are concerned, Conte's position is clear. He said, "I still think there is rampant use of drugs out there. It can be cleaned up but they have to use people from the other side like Dwain and myself, and the knowledge we've gained. I want to be part of the solution."

How is the IOC responding to the prevalence of drugs in the Olympics? We have seen that it has banned athletes from various countries in the run up to the Games. However, sports writers in the United States have been even more critical of the ethos of the Games. Filip Bondy wrote in the *Daily News*, "The Olympic games have been synonymous with drugs, politics, pollution, nationalism and corrupt judging—one vice for every ring."

Whether the Olympics can retain their former innocence, free and untainted from drugs remains to be seen.

Section-IV

The Racial Divide

Chapter-21

Black on Black Violence

We live in an age of the no-parent family. It is Saturday night and the guns are out. Daylight will be greeted by muggings and people will be stabbed and shot. There are those who will be at the wrong place at the wrong time. Mothers and daughters will wail and tell us about the good qualities of those killed. In the recent *Daily News* feature, one parent was moved to say, "you know things are getting hard if you say, thank god my child was only wounded".

The newspaper went on to document really tragic two days for the black community. On the weekend of 28 May 2008, there were five separate incidents that involved shootings. On Monday, a 20-year old man was shot in the chest in Lennox Avenue on West 133rd Street. An hour later, six people were shot in Marcus Garvey Park. These were followed by three more shootings in separate incidents.

While it is heartening to note that crime has dropped in New York City, the shootings described bring little comfort to those affected. The details of the violence leave scars on the individuals and their community as well. For example, 15-year old Dejanay Dawson was screaming on Harlem Street as she fled gunshots at a Memorial Day barbecue. As it turned out, Dejanay was 1 of 10 persons who was shot in gunfire in Harlem that weekend. According to Dejanay, "My friends were screaming. There was blood all over me... the bullet was right up my scalp. I could've died." A man who was seen ditching a semi-automatic handgun was arrested. He is only 15-year old.

The statistics for major crimes in a two-year period are most revealing. In 2007, there were 172 murders for the first half of that year. In the first half of 2008, there were 190 murders which represent a 10 per cent increase. Felony assault, grand larceny, and grand larceny auto have dropped only marginally while robbery has increased by five per cent from 7,550 in 2007 to 7,902 in 2008. Rape has also increased by 8 per cent while shootings have increased by 10 per cent. In fairness, not all of these crimes can be pinned on the black community. However, the incidence of black crime is so worrying that black leaders have spoken out on the issue.

Reverend Al Sharpton has called for a summit to discuss the crime situation in the black community and to suggest ways and means to deal pro-actively with the problem. Social commentators have also begun to give their interpretation as to why the crime rate in the black community is getting out of control. One cause is that the streets are flooded with illegal handguns. Police Commissioner Raymond Kelly has stated that "the shootings in Harlem are evidence of the apparent ease with which teens are able to acquire illegal guns and to use them without regard to consequences".

Mayor Michael Bloomberg has stated that "although New York remains the big city in America, I know that's a small solace to anyone who has personally been affected by a serious crime." The statements by two public officials highlight the growing crime situation and the need for urgent action to be taken.

In his State of the Union Address in 2005, President George Bush appeared to recognize the need for action. He pledged to allocate 150 million dollars to educate young people about the need to prevent violence. This was well-intentioned but not enough to stop the gunplay on the city streets. Earl Hutchinson, writing in 2006, remarked, "Despite the pet theories of liberals and conservatives, blacks aren't killing each other because they are violent or crime-prone by nature, because they are poor and oppressed, or even because they are acting out the obscene violence they see and hear on TV, films, and in gangster rap lyrics." What could be the reason for the violence?

There is an on-going debate as to whether the lyrics in rap music demean women and are insensitive to the needs of the black community. Reverend Clyde Butts has argued that rap music with offensive lyrics should not be tolerated. This view is supported by columnist Stanley Crouch and others, who feel that black youth can do well to bypass CDs that have offensive lyrics. In fact, Reverend Butts organized a campaign some years ago to publicly burn CDs with lyrics that demean women. While it is difficult to link offensive lyrics to the recent crime wave, keeping songs clean will be a major step in rethinking strategies for moving forward.

Reverend Al Sharpton is more of a realist than the theoretician Earl Hutchinson. Reverend Sharpton points out that, "Last year, in 2007, nearly one black child a day under the age of 17 was shot and killed in New York City. Shot mostly by other black city residents." He has proposed a summit on violence in a few weeks, the purpose of which would be to suggest workable solutions to the crime situation.

There are those who feel that the situation is already out of control and little can be done to stop it. Teachers and guidance counselors, for instance, would like parents to exert greater influence in the lives of their children. There are too many children who are hardened by the streets and who are members of gangs at a young age. Some parents assume only an absentee role in the lives of their children. They are too stressed and too busy to enforce rules of the home. In a good many cases, there are no rules and the child is left to fend for him or herself.

Violence is glorified in our society. Recently, two articles written by personalities in the black community address the question of violence. Errol Louis writing in the Daily News was critical of the impact of 'gangsta music'. Louis upbraided Deejay Don Imus for insulting the black women athletes of Rutgers University. He also commented on the rift between Curtis (50 Cent) Jackson and Kanye West. Apparently, Curtis Jackson won't be retiring after all even though Kanye West has outsold him.

But more importantly, it was the lyrics in the songs that concerned Errol Louis. The use of the N-word and profanities and the impression that anything goes creates a license for black youths to venture into areas of deviance. The R&B legend Nona Henryx has some advice for young black artists. She wants them to take a business course, to control their images, lyrics, and publishing and distribution rights. This may prevent them from being pushed into using degrading lyrics.

Another piece of advice has come from Fate Jenkins, a former black beauty queen. Ms Jenkins refers to the movement in a small

Louisiana town where a black person can be fined for exposing his/her undergarments. According to Ms Jenkins, "Those who want to ban sagging pants are onto something and its more than just about indecency. It's about your self image as young black men and our self image as African Americans. Ms Jenkins said that the sagging pants trend started in America's prisons, where inmates were not allowed to wear belts or have shoe laces. Before long, the gangsta-rap world caught on and made the look a symbol of street life in urban communities across America, New York City included."

This brings us to the central question and that is: what can be done to stop violence in the black community? The answer is not clear-cut or simple. Black leaders recognize that black-on-black crime is a problem and have suggested a summit to discuss the matter. A summit alone will not solve crime but it is a good start. There are other steps that will have to be taken, including parental responsibility, strong family values, and a commitment to education.

Chapter-22

Blacks Built the Capitol

America is up to its neck in debt. The government is split along party lines. Politics has been given a bad name. There is waste and the government is doing little to tackle it. Race has become a divisive issue and is at the heart of the debate regarding the future of America. In decision-making, Washington is suffering from the influence of the lobbyists and "backroom politics". This sounds strikingly familiar today. But this was the description of America in 1790, only 14 years after the War of Independence.

Two hundred years later, some of the same issues of 1790 can be found in our country. On his first day in power, President Barack Obama imposed rules to curb wage increases and the influence of lobbyists. After the pomp and fanfare of the inauguration of President Obama, it is important that we pause and take stock of the current situation. The present is tied to the past. As President Obama stood in the Capitol and spoke to millions, history came full circle.

During the inauguration, the Capitol was resplendent. Washington looked like a giant promenade on which thousands stood to witness history. In the old days, slaves were bought and sold not far from where Presidents take the oath. The National Archives was formerly a slave market. Lincoln Park was founded in 1876 by freed slaves. It was Charlotte Scott who donated the first five dollars she earned as a free woman to build the park in the name of Lincoln.

The Capitol was built by slave labor. It was their blood, sweat and tears that made the White House white. George Washington wanted an imperial city with grand architecture. He wanted it to be finished quickly. If he failed, the capital of the United States would be returned to Philadelphia. The agreement to establish America's capital on the Potomac was a result of a deal between Thomas Jefferson, Alexander Hamilton and James Madison. The First Secretary of the US Treasury was Alexander Hamilton who was born on the Caribbean island of Nevis.

Hamilton rose to become one of the most influential persons in the United States of America before he fell to the bullet of Aaron Burr. The influence of the Caribbean was also prominent in the design of the Capitol building. These designs were drawn by William Thorton, a slave-owning abolitionist from the island of Tortola. The completion of the Capitol became a personal obsession of George Washington. He had the vision that the Capitol would become a great highway and a metropolis. But what was the role of blacks in the completion of the Capitol? It is well known that Benjamin Banneker was responsible for much of the architectural drawings of the Capitol. He was also famous for the many uses of peanuts and almanacs.

According to historians, over a period of 70 years, slaves worked from dawn to dusk to make the nations capital a reality. They cleaned trenches and brush for the Mall and the Boulevards in Washington. They did not receive a fair day's pay. However, the Germans and Irish immigrants were paid the princely sum of between 5 and 10 dollars a week for their labor.

On any given day, slaves could be found in quarries digging trenches and ditches, pulling timber, cutting stones, and doing other manual work. Virginia was the largest slave holding state before the Civil War with a slave population of over 400,000. Maryland had a slave population of 100,000 while the district of Columbia had 3,000 slaves. It is generally agreed that the Capitol was built by a workforce that comprised slave labor.

The slaves were responsible for hauling bricks and for building foundations and walls. The lumber that were felled and sawed by slaves have held up the Capitol to this day. Where did the slaves come from? According to various records, they came from houses and farms in Virginia, Maryland and a district of Columbia. On the Capitol dome, there is an imposing 9 feet 6 inch statue. This is symbolic of freedom. How was the dome built? Its construction is part of a rich and fascinating story.

The plastic cast for the dome was cut in pieces in Rome but the trick was to fit the pieces and "bronze" them so that it could be hoisted onto the building. In order to accomplish this delicate operation, a slave named Phillip Reid figured out how to apply the bronze to the plaster. The story of Phillip Reid belongs to the tradition of great American biographies. Reid's ancestors were Yorubas from Africa. They took pride in sculpture and metal casting. Reid was purchased as a slave by Clark Mills. He was the owner of a foundry that was given the contract to caste the statue of freedom on the capitol dome. The full-sized plaster model was completed in Rome by Thomas Crawford in 1856. In April 1858, the model left Rome for America on the ship 'Emily Taylor'. The ship sprung a leak over the Atlantic and the statue had to be transferred to another ship in Bermuda.

The freedom statue was then transferred to Mills Foundry in Maryland but the workers there went on strike for higher wages. Time was running out for the installation. Clark Mills then turned to the slave who had been working alongside the foreman. He was Phillip Reid. The remaining casting of the statue was done in five sections, each weighing over a ton.

Under Reid's supervision, the work was successfully completed and the statue was transported from Maryland to Washington in 1863. On 2 December 1863, the statue of freedom was hoisted to the top of Capitol dome in the midst of great celebration. There was even a 23-gun salute to mark the event. The Capitol dome remains today the most prominently placed symbol of all in Washington and a testament to the contributions of slave labor to American heritage.

Chapter-23

Caribbean Blacks in America

One open door can lead to another. In 1872, Victoria Woodhull created history. She became the first woman to run for President of the United States. At that time, Victoria was one of the most famous persons in the country. She was nominated by the Equal Right's Party and her running-mate was Frederick Douglass, the black abolitionist. Douglass went on to become President Lincoln's first ambassador to Haiti. One hundred years later, history of another kind was written.

In 1972, Shirley Chisholm became the first black woman to seek the Presidency of the United States. She credited Victoria Woodhull for taking up the mantle for women and all those who wanted equality. At the Democratic Convention in Miami, she explained that she was running for President because one day, "others will feel themselves as capable of running for high political office as any wealthy, good looking white male". If only Shirley Chisholm was around on 20 January 2009.

Shirley Chisholm was a product of the Caribbean. Indeed, Caribbean blacks have played a pivotal role in uplifting the consciousness of mainstream America. They have redirected the issues and concerns that confront America to policymakers so that laws can be written to redress injustice. Shirley Chisholm was in the forefront of the struggle for equality and justice. She was born on 30 November 1924 in Brooklyn, New York. Her father was from Guyana and her mother was from Barbados.

Shirley was sent to Barbados for her early education. She praised the British-style education in Barbados for its discipline and for her early upbringing. Shirley graduated from Brooklyn College in sociology and later from Columbia University in child psychology. She married Conrad Chisholm, a Jamaican, in 1949 and together they became involved in local politics. The focal point in their campaign was that minorities needed to be mobilized.

In 1960, Shirley founded the Unity Democratic Club, the purpose of which was to organize minorities and to fight for better facilities in the district. Her efforts paid off handsomely when in 1964 she was elected to a State Assembly seat. She supported and won funding for child-care facilities and for schools. In 1968, Chisholm won a seat in Congress and served on the Education and Labor Committees.

A seat in Congress became a springboard for her to run for President in 1972. She did not win but 151 of the delegates voted for her, which was no mean achievement in those days. Shirley Chisholm paved the way for others, including Jesse Jackson and Barack Obama.

Another Caribbean personality who made a major impact in New York was Bertram Baker. He was from Nevis. This island is famous for another son Alexander Hamilton who became the first Secretary of the Treasury. Bertram Baker became the first black to be elected in New York. He won a seat to the New York State Assembly in 1948. While in the assembly, he wrote laws to ban discrimination based on race. A great honor to come his way was in 1966 when he was appointed by majority whip of the state assembly. This happened to be the highest position achieved by a black politician at the time.

Baker's interest was not only confined to politics. He was also the executive secretary of the American Tennis Association. The ATA helped to clear the way for players such as Althea Gibson to succeed. It is interesting to note that Baker's granddaughter Diane Patrick ran for office in Boston and attributed her success to her 'firebrand' grandfather.

One of the most celebrated blacks from the Caribbean to live in the United States was Marcus Garvey. He is a national hero of Jamaica. His life was one of action and ideas and some of them ran counter to the period in which he lived. Garvey was born on 17 August 1887 in St. Ann's Bay, Jamaica. He died in London in 1940 at the relatively young age of 52. Garvey's central message was that black people needed to redeem Africa. He became convinced of this idea based on his travels to Europe and Latin America.

By the time he reached America in 1916, he had begun to promote the idea that "it was essential to unite all people of African ancestry of the world to one great body to establish a country and absolute government of their own". Garvey traveled extensively in the United States and by August 1920, his Universal Improvement Association (UNIA) had a membership of four million people. At its international convention that month, more than 25,000 persons listened to Garvey's speech at Madison Square Garden.

Garvey proposed Liberia as the country of black repatriation and resettlement. This idea was abandoned when business interests in Liberia opposed it. In the meantime, two powerful forces were against Garvey. Some black intellectuals in the United States saw Garvey's campaign as mischievous. Scholar WEB Du Bois, for instance, called Garvey "a dangerous enemy of the Negro race, who was either a lunatic or a traitor".

The FBI, under J Edgar Hoover, wanted to deport Garvey to Jamaica. When a mail charge of fraud stuck, Garvey's stay in the United States were numbered. He was jailed but was eventually pardoned by President Calvin Coolidge. Marcus Garvey was deported to Jamaica in November 1925.

The greatest accolade to be bestowed on Garvey was on a warm day in Jamaica in June 1965. Dr Martin Luther King and his wife Coretta were visiting the island. They laid a wreath at the grave of Marcus Garvey. Dr King was moved to say, "Marcus Garvey was the first man of color to develop a mass movement. He was the first man on a mass scale and level to give millions of Negroes a sense of dignity and destiny. And make the Negro feel he was somebody."

Today, there are schools and colleges named after him. It is suggested that the 'Black Star' in the center of the flag of Ghana was inspired by Garvey. Apart from Chisholm, Baker, and Garvey, there are countless blacks of Caribbean origin who have made tangible contributions to America. Constance Baker Motley helped to write the laws to end segregation in schools. Her parents were from Nevis. General Colin Powell was the US Secretary of State and his parents were from Jamaica. The present Governor of New York, David Paterson, is of Jamaican and Grenadian ancestry.

New Yorkers will note that Una Clarke from Jamaica won a seat in the City Council and her daughter Yvette is in the US House of Representatives. In 1953, Hulan E Jack from St. Lucia became the first black to be elected as Manhattan Borough President. The current President of the Borough of Queens is Helen Marshall who was born in Guyana.

We should salute the contributions that blacks from the Caribbean are making to America. They have greatly enriched the quality of life in the United States and will continue to do so for many more years.

Chapter-24

Elizabeth Jennings: A Streetcar for Freedom

In those days, the drivers carried whips. Those who were deemed undesirables would be beaten and forced to leave the buses. This practice was quite common in New York, but in 1854, one woman had the courage to stand up and change the system. Change usually comes from conviction and a desire to fight for what is right. When Elizabeth Jennings boarded the omnibus at the corner of Pearl and Chatham Streets, little did she know that she would rewrite history books.

It was high summer and the 24-year old school teacher was on her way to church where she was an organist. In the 1840s, blacks were not allowed to use public transportation. The alternative was walking since the 'colored buses' hardly worked. By 1850, the administration had not decided as to whether blacks could ride the omnibuses. An omnibus was a horse drawn bus or a horse drawn street car. The refusal to transport African-Americans at times provoked threats of legal action, but this was considered a joke by the establishment. Who could take on the city and win?

Elizabeth Jennings came from a well-connected family that was involved in a movement to end discrimination. This was based mainly in the church. Her father, Thomas Jennings, joined preachers such as JWC Pennington, Henry Garnet, Peter S Ewell and Peter Porter. This group would meet regularly to discuss ways and means to improve the condition of blacks in the city. Reverend Pennington, in particular, was vehemently opposed to segregation and his sermons at the First Colored Congregational Church were used to promote equal rights. No one knew that history was about to be made when on 16 July 1864, Elizabeth Jennings boarded an omnibus to play the organ at her church.

Manhattan's pre-Civil War climate had more than a hint of radicalism. Although many people followed the "rules", buses with the sign "colored persons allowed" were a symbol of separateness in a city with the nations' largest African-American population. As was common in those days, the bus driver would use his authority to decide who should be on the bus. On that July day, Elizabeth Jennings was seen as an easy target. As soon as he saw her, the driver refused to let her on, claiming that the bus was full. When she pointed out that it was in fact the opposite, the driver went on the defensive. Jennings was told that the other passengers were uncomfortable by her presence. She did not accept this explanation. She insisted on her rights to ride the bus, but the driver took her by her hand and tried to forcibly eject her.

According to the *New York Tribune*, "Elizabeth Jennings resisted. The conductor got her down on the platform, jammed her bonnet, soiled her dress, and injured her person. Quite a crowd gathered, but she eventually resisted. Finally, after the car had gone on further, with the aid of a policemen, they succeeded in removing her."

As can be expected, the community was angry and upset. A rally was called outside the first Colored Congregational Church. There were angry speeches by community leaders. Ms Jennings had stated what had happened on the bus in a letter. She said that as a "respectable person born in New York City" she had no right to be treated like that. She described the driver as a "good for nothing, impudent fellow" who had insulted a decent person on her way to church. Jennings then took the bold and unusual step to sue the bus company, the driver, and the conductor. In the 1850s, it was unthinkable for African-Americans to use the courts to win civil rights. This case attracted immense interest.

The black community began to mobilize itself for the impending court case by publicizing the event. It denounced racism and urged the people to remain calm. Jennings was represented by a young attorney, Chester A Arthur. His involvement in the case was to prove extremely beneficial as Chester Arthur went on to become the 21st President of the United States, following the death of James Garfield in 1881.

In 1815, Brooklyn became a separate city. The case against the Third Avenue Railway Cany took place at Brooklyn's Circuit Court with George William Rockwell presiding. After lengthy summations, the judge ruled in favor of Elizabeth Jennings. It was a historic decision tempered only by the wording of the ruling. According to the judge, "Colored persons, if sober, well behaved and free from disease had the same rights as others, and could neither be excluded by any rules of the Company, nor by any force of violence." This appears to be a rather grudging and demeaning ruling since it cast African-Americans as boisterous, unruly and unclean. But the message was clear. Desegregation on the buses was a thing of the past. African-Americans had won a major victory in New York. Her case was publicized by Frederick Douglass in his newspaper.

Elizabeth Jennings was awarded $500 in damages. However, she did not get the full amount. Some members of the jury "had peculiar notions as to colored peoples rights". Consequently, she was awarded $225 plus $22.50 for court costs. By 1860, all of New York's street and rail cars were desegregated. Elizabeth Jennings went on to marry Charles Graham and to continue teaching in African-American schools. Jennings was to make another impact on American history, when in 1863, a resolution was passed that allowed wealthy New Yorkers to buy their way out of the Civil War draft.

This resolution caused resentment and anger and there was rioting in New York that lasted four days. It was reported that more than 70 blacks were killed. Unfortunately, Jennings' young son died of convulsions during the riots. As the rioting continued, Elizabeth Jennings Graham and her husband managed to get their son to the Greenwood Cemetery in Brooklyn for a proper burial. Elizabeth Jennings was a determined woman whose actions helped to change an ugly law in New York's history. Her unflappable and unyielding courage would go on to inspire a host of other women. Sojourner Truth (1797–1883) fought against slavery and for the rights of women while Harriet Tubman (1823–1913) laid plans for slaves to be free with the Underground Railroad. Mary McLeod Bethune (1875–1955) believed in the role of education as an agent of change and spent much of her life equipping schools with the necessary curriculums to include stories about slavery.

In the political sphere, granting women the right to vote was always going to be resisted by the establishment, but the efforts of Susan B Anthony (1820–1906) and others led to a change in the law. The 19th Amendment in 1920 made it possible for women to vote.

On a chilly day in 2005, the world gathered to pay their respects to Rosa Parks. It was Parks who had refused to give up her seat on a bus in Montgomery, Alabama, in 1955 that led to changes in that city's transit system. Her actions also resulted in the civil rights movement in which Martin Luther King was to play a prominent role.

But America needs to remember a young black school teacher, who, a 100 years before Rosa Parks, refused to bend to the might of the system. In 1830, when the first omnibus routes were established, black New Yorkers were told in *The Colored American*, "Brethren, you are MEN—if you have not horses and vehicles of your own to travel with, stay at home or travel on foot rather than be degraded and insulted on city coaches."

In 1854, Elizabeth Jennings lit a powerful torch that continues to burn brightly today for liberty and justice.

Chapter-25

Harassment of Sikhs Must Stop

He might not have known it at the time but USA also stands for the United Sikhs of America. In 1459, on the banks of Punjab, a most wonderful event took place. A young man, Guru Nanak, decided that the world could be a better place without strife and divisions. His vision was one of a community in which people with Godlike qualities would rule the world. When this happened, there would be no more wars and everyone will live in perpetual peace and happiness. Guru Nanak, with this simple philosophy, became the founder of Sikhism, the fifth largest religion of the world. Sikhism numbers over 25 million members found in all parts of the world. In New York, there are over 100,000 Sikhs and this number is ever-growing.

Sikhs are hardworking, devoted to their families and live for their gurudwara, or temple. They add to the diversity and tapestry for which America is famous. In May 2005, Niall McKay and Marissa Aroy won the Emmy for their documentary *Sikhs in America* which was the culmination of years of research into the lifestyles of an extraordinary group of people. The program showed Sikhs to be dynamic, positive and a worthwhile addition to the culture of America. Recently, Sikhs have been busy making donations to places ravaged by earthquakes and other natural disasters, notably Myanmar.

There are 10 gurus in Sikhism starting with Guru Nanak and ending with Guru Gobind Singh. When Guru Gobind died, the Guruship was passed to the *Guru Granth Sahib*, the Holy Scripture for Sikhs that contains the divine message and has been enforced since. During indentureship, thousands of immigrants left India for Guyana, Trinidad and Suriname and other Caribbean countries. A sizeable portion of Sikhs crossed the Atlantic, taking with them their culture. A few years ago, India sent a distinguished Sikh scholar, Dr Gopal Singh, as High Commissioner to Guyana.

The first Sikhs landed in Canada in 1897 and were given the right to vote in 1947. The first Gurudwara or temple was built in the United States in 1912 in California. In the ensuing years, Sikhs have contributed richly to America, living peacefully among its peoples and practicing their culture without imposing it on anyone. On the basis of reports from the media and from personal experiences of the Sikh community, their tolerance has been met with animosity and violence by elements within the wider population. The statistics are hardly comforting. In the New York area, the treatment meted out to our Sikh brothers and sisters is simply atrocious.

In the public school system, 41 per cent of Sikh children have reported that they have been called derogatory names. For every five students, three have been harassed because they wear turbans or *patkas,* while 25 per cent of New York Sikhs believe they have been racially profiled because of their identity. There are also complaints that Punjabi language translations are not provided at hospitals or other government agencies.

Over 50 per cent of Sikh immigrants have no access to health care or insurance.

As far as employment is concerned, more than one in ten say they have been refused employment and promotion because of their ethnicity. Recently, the public school system in New York was in headlines when reports of brutality against Sikhs were featured. In May 2007, the New York Police Department reported that a Sikh student at Newtown High School in Elmhurst was attacked and had his hair forcibly cut by another student. As part of their beliefs, Sikhs do not cut their hair or shave their faces, which means that their identity is visible.

There can be little doubt that the events of 11 September 2001 have given greater visibility to Sikhs, but unfortunately this has been in a negative manner. For instance, days after the terrorist attacks, Sikhs were abused and even killed as they were mistaken for terrorists. In the five years after 11 September 2001, there were over 500 cases of discrimination that were reported to have taken place against Sikhs.

In May 2008, Sarab Singh of Santa Fe, New Mexico, complained of abuse by the police there apparently for a traffic offense. Sarab Singh argued that the police made up their minds to arrest him once they saw he was a Sikh. Three years ago in Richmond Hill, New York, a Sikh was beaten up by a group of revelers at a catering hall. The judge ruled that it was a biased crime and those responsible were prosecuted.

But it is in schools that most abuse and bias is taking place. In June 2007, four New York City Council members joined members of the Sikh community to release a document called *Hatred in the Hallways*. The report found that "three out of four Sikh boys who go to school in

Queens have been teased or harassed on account of their racial identity". What is even more damaging is the fact that over 40 per cent of Sikh students who wear turbans have been subjected to "some form of discrimination, either hitting, punching or disrespectful touching of the head."

Councilman John Liu led the initiative to write to the Department of Education on behalf of the Sikh Coalition; a move that received support from a wide cross-section of the community. In 2007, the Sikh Coalition produced a report (www.sikhcoalition.org) in order to inform the community on the status of relationships. Unfortunately, neither the report nor the *Hatred in the Hallways* document has been able to put a stop to abuse and discrimination. At Richmond Hill High School in Queens, New York, an 18-year old Sikh student was attacked by a 15-year old in June 2008. This happened after assurances were given by the Department of Education that future occurrences would be stopped.

Where do we go from here? We must not sit back and tolerate attacks on any community. When people are subjected to attacks because of their ethnicity, it affects us all. Tomorrow it could be someone else. Bullies should never be given a free ride. One of the best ways to start the process of acceptance and tolerance is through education. The schools should teach multiculturalism, including lessons on Sikh culture in the early grades as well as in the high schools.

The Sikh Coalition is doing a great job in creating awareness about intolerance but the coalition should be assisted by the wider community, the rank and file to stamp out discrimination by reporting them. Sikhs have descended from a great culture and the United States of America is lucky to have this dynamic and hardworking people in its midst. If one needs any reminder of the brilliance of Sikhs, then one has to look no further than India. The current Prime Minister, Oxford graduate, Manmohan Singh is a Sikh.

Chapter-26

Race Hate in Suffolk County

Suffolk County is poisoned. Racial hatred has overtaken the entire county. It is difficult to imagine that Suffolk County is in New York and that racism in a most destructive way exists there today. In the last few months, a series of incidents have occurred in Suffolk County that leaves one wondering whether this nation has made any progress at all in terms of racial understanding. What is worrying is that race hate has infected the young and when this happens, it makes it extremely difficult to move back the barriers that cloud good judgment. It also makes it impossible to roll out the carpet and welcome tolerance and respect. How did race hate become such a pernicious blot on Suffolk County that immigrant bashing is commonplace and murder can take place based on skin color?

In January 2009, the Riverhead School District in New York charged three high school students with hate crimes. According to a report, "They publicly taunted two of their African-American classmates as they muzzled and handcuffed the hands and feet of a black doll while they strangled its neck with a noose, hanging from ropes from their hands as they imagined the object to be dead." This act was described as incontestably villainous in view of America's history with slavery and segregation. The students involved in perpetrating the crime were given a 15-day jail sentence and the crime was lowered to a second-degree harassment. In order to be clear on what the law has to say on second-degree harassment, it is necessary to quote the relevant legislation.

The New York Hate Crimes Act of 2000 states that a second-degree harassment crime is "to strike, shove, kick or otherwise subject another person to physical contact, or attempt to threaten to do the same because of a belief or perception regarding such person's race, color, national origin, ancestry, gender, religion, religious practice, age, disability or sexual orientation. The Hate Crimes Act then covers a broad area in its definition of harassment. Thus the offence committed by the students on the African-American students is one in a long list that occurs frequently in the United States. What makes Suffolk County special is that for the last 10 years, a climate of fear has pervaded the county that is fueled by race hate.

Research by the Southern Poverty Law Center has revealed that racial hatred in Suffolk County has been mainly directed at the Hispanic community. The cases are too many to highlight but some of the most infamous ones will be mentioned to show that discrimination based on skin color has no place in the United States of America. In June 1999, a car swerved into a Mexican construction worker and knocked him to the ground. Two men climbed out of the car with baseball bats and called the man "spic" and "wetback". A police report was filed but no arrest was made. On 14 September 2000, the County Legislature passed a resolution requesting that the US Immigration and Naturalization Service should "aggressively enforce the federal deportation laws".

A month later, a construction worker from Honduras was assaulted by a group of teenagers in Farmingville. The attack was unprovoked, the victim's nose was broken but no one was arrested. On 17 September 2000, Regan Wagner and Christopher Slavin lured two Mexican day laborers, Israel Perez and Magdaleno Estrada Escamilla, to an abandoned building after promising them that they will get work. The men were attacked with crowbar, shovel and knife. They escaped. In a court hearing, Wagner made a statement. He said that he "wanted to beat up someone after a long night of alcohol and drugs had made him angry". Wagner was sentenced to 15 years and Slavin to 25 years for the attack. The Sachem Quality of Life (SQL), an anti-immigrant group, in response to the sentencing called Perez and Estrada "criminals". On 22 September 2000, a new group Brookhaven Citizens for Peaceful Solution was formed to reduce racial tensions but the SQL wanted no part in it.

Violence continued to escalate in Suffolk County. Franco Carnero, a Latino immigrant, was attacked in Patchogue by a dozen white teens wielding baseball bats. No one was arrested. In July 2001, the Long Island Immigrant Alliance was formed. But this did not prevent Alejandro Castillo, an immigrant from Ecuador, from being kicked by four teenagers who wanted his green card. Castillo needed plates in his skull after the attack. But again no one was charged.

On 4 November 2003, one of the most important landmarks in race relations in Suffolk County took place. It was on this date that Steve Levy, Democrat, and anti-immigrant hardliner, was elected as Suffolk County Chief Executive. Steve went to work quickly. On

29 November 2003, he proposed that "some county police officers should be given the power to detain for possible deportation any undocumented immigrant detained on other charges". The local unions rejected Levy's proposals because it was felt that it might be difficult to administer and tensions will be ignited.

The *New York Times* reported that in 2006 three Latino teenagers were lured into a shed in East Hampton by Neo-Nazi skinheads and were threatened and terrorized with threats of "white power". Racial attacks continued well into 2007 almost on a month-to-month basis. In 2008, there was no letting up as attacks on Latinos became more relentless. On 11 July 2008, Mario Lopez, an Ecuadorian immigrant, was attacked by eight teenagers. His eyes were sprayed with a chemical and he was kicked and beaten. A similar fate met Carlos Orellano a few days later in Patchogue.

The calls for racial tolerance in Suffolk County appeared to fall on deaf ears. Many of those who wanted dialogue with the county administration saw Chief Executive Steve Levy as the stumbling block. In 2005, he refused to meet with immigration advocates stating emphatically, "I'm not one who's going to be intimidated by their antics or marches. Bring it on." He saw these groups as a one per cent fringe. Did the official response to the anti-immigrant feeling lead to unchecked racism and hatred? Human rights groups appear to think so, especially after the Lucero incident on 8 November 2008.

Marcello Lucero, a 37-year old Ecuadorian immigrant, was stabbed to death allegedly by a group of seven teenagers who called themselves the "Caucasian Crew". The stabbing happened in Patchogue. As if this was not dangerous enough, another Hispanic man was attacked the same day by allegedly some of the same teens. What was the response of the County Executive? Steve Levy told reporters that it was because of his anti-immigrant stand that the Lucero murder "was blown out of proportion". Levy further said that if the murder was committed elsewhere, it would have been "a one-day story".

There is no doubt that these incidents have created a climate of fear and distrust in Suffolk County. Why do Hispanics flock there? The county is a place in which there is a concentration of wealth. For example, the seaside community known as 'the Hamptons' is a most expensive zip code in the nation, with a median home sale price of about three million dollars. In view of the entrenched racism that exists in Suffolk County, what can be done to promote tolerance on both sides?

The Southern Poverty Law Center documented many cases of racism in Suffolk County. It found that race-hate is fueled by officials who are supposed to protect the people. For example, one county official said that if he were to see Latino laborers, he would "be out with baseball bats". Another said that he would "unload his gun and start shooting, period". When this reaction comes from those who are in positions of authority, the situation can only get worse. As a start, local politicians should tone down their language and use words that seek reconciliation and tolerance. Secondly, a person's immigration status should not be requested if he or she makes a report of a crime or becomes a witness. But equally important Steve Levy and his county officers should be required to undergo sensitivity training.

The cases of harassment against Latinos are too numerous for them to be coincidental. The language used by key members of the county administration has been inflammatory. Violence has not helped the cause of those that seek tolerance and respect. Dialogue is urgently needed, as a start, to stop the unwarranted attacks on immigrants in Suffolk County.

Section-V

Economic Indicators

Chapter-27

Corporate Greed

When will this madness stop? When will greed give way to honesty and those simple values will reign again? We live in a world in which smart means that a person has to be devious. It hardly matters where one lives. These days the science of getting over, of pulling the wool over decency and morality is seen as a triumph and an achievement. In these difficult times, there are families that are struggling to make ends meet. Their budgets are hardly enough to pay for rent, food, fuel and the other bills. Most families live a decent life, preferring to play by the rules and to set a good example to their children, even if they live on a shoestring.

In the corporate world, it's a different story. It is not only a dog-eat-dog society, but it is one in which wealth is accumulated and measured by how many exorbitant deals one can make. The bigger the deals the greater the bonuses will be for top executives. Can we really afford the multi-million dollar bonuses given to executives of corporations?

In 2006, matters came to a head when this very question was asked by angry shareholders at two Fortune 500 companies.

When the shareholders met at the Home Depot and Exxon

Mobile Corp, they made it clear that they were fed up with business as usual. At the Home Depot meeting that was held in Delaware, the CEO attempted to shift the debate away from the payment of salaries to top members of the corporations. It was alleged that the CEO in question stifled the debate about his 245 million dollars in salary and benefits. What was the response of the directors of the company?

According to reports, they shut down the meeting and did not entertain further discussions. At the Exxon meeting in Dallas, shareholders interviewed management and inquired about the retirement package of the former CEO Lee Raymond. He is said to have received 70 million dollars as salary in 2005 and cash payout of 98 million dollars. *The Washington Post* reports that a vice president at that meeting described Raymond's package as "colossal greed".

Comcast is the largest cable company in the United States. But the corporation has a history of discrimination against unionized employees. Its CEO has "one third of the voting power of all Comcast shares even though he owns less than three per cent of the total outstanding equity." In 2003, Brian Roberts, the CEO, was alleged to have received 20 million dollars in compensation and an additional 34 million in excised stock options.

Comcast rates went up shortly afterwards.

It is agreed that the tax laws are so complex that the CEOs are able to get away with scandalous sums of money legally. President Barack Obama in his appearance on the 'Jay Leno Show' stated that the big sums of money paid to AIG employees were not illegal. However, in principle and practice, they are reprehensible in the eyes of most of America. The Institute of Policy Studies states that the tax breaks are cooked up in Washington and the executives and their companies can enjoy at least 20 billion dollars a year on income tax breaks. The IPS states further that "every household filing a return pays about 192 dollars extra in taxes to cover these breaks". It is interesting to note that in 1970, the average annual salary of a CEO was about 30 times the pay of an average worker. Today, that has increased to 344 times to 11 million dollars a year.

But this is not all. In 2008, the brokerage units of financial companies in New York is reported to have lost in the excess of 35 billion dollars. This loss should have resulted in financial prudence and cost-cutting, but this was hardly the case. New York State Comptroller reports that these companies paid approximately 19 billion dollars in bonuses which happens to be the sixth largest on record. The Press Secretary of the White House, Robert Gibbs, has described these payouts as "outrageous".

There were more outrageous practices that are mind-boggling. At a time when the economy is in such poor shape, the irresponsibility of the Wall Street could not be more dramatic. John Thain is a former CEO of Merrill Lynch. As he announced his resignation from the Bank of America, the news broke that he had spent more than one million dollars redecorating his office. He paid 800,000 dollars for a celebrity designer and 87,000 dollars for a rug.

These practices have left the Obama administration in a state of exasperation. Citigroup, for example, had received 45 billion dollars in Tarp funds. Citi decided buying a private jet for 50 million dollars, but the Obama administration had to pull the purchase. The American Insurance Group (AIG) scandal has become the most unpalatable pill for the public to swallow. AIG recently reported that it had accrued losses to the extent of 61.7 billion dollars for the fourth quarter of 2008. This makes it the largest corporate loss in history.

The speaker of the House, Nancy Pelosi, made her comments quite clear when she heard the news. She said, "I call upon the executives of the AIG to right the wrong they have done to American taxpayers who are footing the bill for the most expensive government rescue in history." President Obama could hardly contain himself as he addressed the AIG issue. At one point, he departed from his script and said, "Excuse me. I am choked up with anger here. This is a corporation that finds itself in corporate distress due to recklessness and greed."

He further said that he had directed the Secretary of the Treasury Timothy Geithner to "pursue every legal avenue to block these bonuses and make the American taxpayer whole".

The bonuses that AIG were paying out totaled 165 million dollars. The question that must be asked is: why do corporations continue to award themselves when the economy is in such a poor shape and when it is clearly known that it is the taxpayer that will foot the bill? Greed is a major part of the answer. These companies seem oblivious to the reality facing the nation. They are accustomed to living the high life and now to ask them to make cuts and changes appear to be impossible for them. Bernie Madoff is in jail but AIG knows that the government will come to its rescue. Shouldn't the government have included regulations about bonuses prior to a bailout plan?

President Obama agrees that this could have been done and has taken steps to correct it.

Chapter-28

Stadiums and Malls

A slice of pizza costs five dollars at the Yankee Stadium. There is also a wide selection of gourmet dishes to excite the palate. It is argued that fans can be so caught up with the frills of the stadium that baseball would be the last thing on their minds. At the new Citi Field Stadium that houses the Mets, another state-of-the-art facility is unveiled. The argument here is that millions are poured into the construction of massive stadiums that local communities are hurting. Stadiums have their supporters but in small town America, stadiums and malls have become 'white elephants' and are actually closing down. According to one writer, "Many malls throughout America have closed due to poor business conditions. It is based on too much for too few. Many of those structures are left to decay and become eyesores. Some have been torn down and were not necessary in the first place."

Are the two new stadiums in New York really necessary? The debate will go on for a long time. When the land space they occupy is considered as well as the impact on local parks and communities are taken into consideration, construction can have a negative impact. It is estimated that a Wall Mart needs 20 acres of land space, while

Home Depot needs 25 acres. When these mega corporations congest in a small area, the result can be harmful to the local community.

The real estate crisis has forced developers with a vision to drastically amend their plans. For example, in 2003, when things were better, the Mayor of Tampa in Florida was singing an upbeat tune. He wanted to transform downtown Tampa into a bustling area with offices, condos, restaurants and bars. A 760 area downtown space would become a hub in which residents would work, shop and play. It was proposed to build 11,000 new condos but the planners did not foresee the housing crisis.

By 2008, only a quarter of the condos were built and the dream has been deferred rather indefinitely. A top real estate broker in Florida said that Tampa had a false start. People made deposits on condos and didn't close. Gone are the days when builders will build and people will buy. The real estate crisis in Florida is expected to deepen and there could well be a second 'Hurricane Katrina' when it hits the market. Nationwide, the business sector is reeling from the loss of jobs. For example, in 2008, over a million jobs were lost and the projections for 2009 were not promising.

Some scholars argue that cities have not lost their luster, but that home-buyers have become scarce. One informed real estate developer states, "We are losing anchor stores and large chains are closing stores and even going out of business altogether." Debt is the pillar of the US economy but who is going to finance it? The US deficit for 2009 was a whopping 1.4 trillion dollars, the biggest since 1945.

One economist predicts, "For those Americans without jobs or whose incomes do not rise with inflation, life will be cruel." How will this affect the retired population? They have not done well so far as the stock market crash reduced their wealth and their remaining assets are not producing wealth. It can be concluded that the vast majority of retirees are living by consuming their capital. What do they have to do with stadiums and malls? The point is that when people lose their jobs and homes are foreclosed, the impact on families can be disastrous. Closing one's wallet will affect the ability of shops to stay open and stadiums to attract fans.

In Staten Island, General Growth Properties he owner of Staten Island Mall, is in danger of going bankrupt After its shares plunged, the stocks of General Growth Properties were removed from the Sand P 500 Index. But the biggest financial crisis to hit America has not stopped three new giant stadiums to be opened in the past weeks. They are the Yankee Stadium, Citi Field, and the Dallas Cowboys. These are three of the most expensive stadiums ever built and their combined cost is over 3.5 billion dollars.

The original plan for Citi Field, the former Shea Stadium, was created as part of the New York City 2012 Olympic bid. The plans also included a retractable roof. As the world knows, New York City lost its bid to host the Olympics. In November 2006, it was announced that Shea would be replaced by Citi Field. This was named after Citigroup Inc. The change of name is not cheap. The agreement is that Citigroup would pay 20 million dollars per year for the naming rights for the next 20 years.

The new Citi Field has been enveloped in controversy. The Willets Point community, for instance, lies in the shadow of the stadium. Community leaders and politicians have pointed out that the needs of

Willets Point have been overlooked in the construction process. They further point out that, "Willets Point is probably the most polluted 60 acres in New York." Some commentators say that Willets Point is unlike the charming neighborhoods of Boston's Fenway Park and London's Wembley Stadium or Wimbledon. According to one writer, "Willets Point has been polluted by destructive government policies and private developing of wastes for over a century, and that today has a threatening, almost feral, ambience. And it is across the street from the Mets Stadium."

Public pressure and media exposure have led the city of New York to intervene. The Bloomberg administration has stated that it is committed to cleaning up the area. As for the Yankee Stadium, the Independent Budget Office states that the cost of replacing 22 acres of South Bronx Parkland has increased by millions of dollars. The report points out, "Design revisions, project additions, unanticipated clean-ups of hazardous materials and construction inflation have driven costs by 76 million dollars." The special boxes that were built for the corporate sector have not to date been snapped up by the business community and the stadium is losing money.

Some economists argue that sports stadium provide no significant monetary benefits. In the long term, the slight increase in income is offset by the stadium financing and operating costs. Since its opening, over 20 home runs have been hit at the Yankee Stadium. At this rate, there could be 365 by the December, which is equivalent to one home run for each day of the year. Is there a design flaw? Would it be better for New York City if those billions were better invested?

Chapter-29

The Mortgage Crisis

Once upon a time, in a leafy street in Brooklyn, Rosa unlocked her dreams. She longed for the day when she could have her own home; her children would have separate rooms; and she would be free from the shackles of rents. Rosa scraped every penny and put it into her savings. There were many real estate brokers to choose from and they all seemed to use the same language. She could buy her home without any down payment or income check or wage slips. She could be pre-qualified over the phone for a mortgage; all she had to do was call a number and sign a few papers. The offers were tempting and Rosa took the plunge to own a piece of her American Dream.

But Rosa had her doubts. She earned a modest income of $1500 a month. How could she afford to make ends meet? She was told by a smiling real estate agent not to worry. He would arrange everything. In the days approaching the closing, and the exchange of contracts, Rosa could think of nothing else. Her new home became an obsession. At the closing, the entire family was present and it turned out to be a big ceremony. Rosa duly moved into her new home and settled in nicely. There were some renovations to do, but those would come in time.

Six months passed and Rosa's dream was abruptly turning into a nightmare. She received a letter from the bank stating that the interest on her mortgage would be doubled to 12 per cent. This meant that she would not be able to pay her bills. Frantic with worry, she was about to lose her home. Her attorneys, real estate broker and even the bank couldn't help. The real estate people told her it was all her fault; she should have read the fine print.

If this description sounds unbelievable, consider the case of Eva Murphy. Her story was reported in the *Daily News* in September 2007. Eva was approached by "2000 Homes" two years ago. They convinced her that she could afford a home. Eva was unemployed at the time. How could she afford to repay the mortgage? It was not a problem she was told. Blank application forms were filled and her income was listed as 9,000 per month.

Eva Murphy lived in Queens and at the time was on welfare. The real estate agent told her she could afford a home even though she had bad credit. He suggested that she bought a home in Roscow Street, in Jamaica, Queens. The selling price was $430,000. At the closing, she found out that the price was actually $538,000. This meant that the repayment which would have been about $2,000 per month had jumped to $3,990 per month.

The mortgage application listed Eva Murphy as the "marketing manager" of a company owned by her husband who was a "loan officer". Eva Murphy could not afford to pay the mortgage and late last year, her house ended up in foreclosure. Eva Murphy is 64-year old and receives about $1,000 per month from social security and workers compensation. Reacting to the news of her income and foreclosure, she said, "I haven't worked since 29 January 1991 and now all of a sudden, I got a job in the diamond industry. I am supposed to be a manager or something. Oh, my God. How did they do that?"

The foreclosure of Eva Murphy's house is only the tip of the downward spiral. In September 2007, State Senator Jeffrey Klein (D-Bronx) found that foreclosures were "rising at an alarming rate" as part of the subprime crisis that is hitting the country. Klein's figures showed 14,561 foreclosures in New York City with 6,000 alone in Queens. These occurred between 1 July 2006 and 31 July 2007.

According to reliable estimates, 8,000 homes in Queens will be foreclosed in the next few months. The mortgage crisis has not only hit New York. In the other states, people are feeling the effects of the mess. In Ohio, for instance, over the past 18 months, foreclosures have hit the suburbs hard. Lawns remain neat and houses are unboarded but the "for sale" sign seems to be up for an eternity. The fact is people are not buying. The case of the Smiths from Cleveland is a reminder of the subprime chaos.

In May 2006, the Smiths put their home on the market. They had no credit problems, never missed a monthly payment or took out a risky mortgage. After a year, they still have had no offers on their house. They even dropped the price of their three colonial bedrooms from $110,000 to $98,000. Mrs Smith said, "My heart panics every time I drive down the street and I see another 'for sale' sign. The competition to sell is just ridiculous."

But back in Queens, in New York City, statistics are equally dismal. It is estimated that 20 per cent of the homes are going into foreclosure. The rates of subprime lender loans in Queens are the highest in minority neighborhoods. It seems that there is no amount of professional ethics that will stop someone from preying on the poor. A disgraceful episode involves a Guyanese attorney who has been charged by the Queens District Attorney for scamming a sick man out of his home.

According to the Queens DA, the attorney and a real estate agent are charged for "carefully orchestrating a real estate scheme that netted them hundred of thousands of dollars in mortgage loan proceeds and involved everything from 'straw' buyers to 'show' checks to help the unsuspecting homeowners from learning the truth—that their homes were being stolen right from under them."

The reality is that a 78-year old Jamaica resident went home from the hospital only to find that his house was sold to someone else illegally. How did this happen? When the owner of the house fell ill, his signature was forged on a deed and his house was sold for $200,000 to a real estate operated by the attorney's brother. He, in turn, sold it to the relative of a real estate agent. The relative transferred the deed to her father and he in turn sold the house for three times its value. The house was 'flipped' a number of times with the sick owner losing his home.

What can be done to help those who are affected? The federal government has been pressed to vote for a monetary bailout but this will take time. In the interim, speaking to those who have been affected and forming support groups will help. But legal counseling is extremely important. In this regard, organizations such as ACORN can be of help. Then there is the Foreclosure Relief Law Project that is also useful.

If you don't get far with these, then contact your local elected representative. Predatory 'angel' lenders are busy planning their next moves. Beware of the tempting offers and 'sweet talk' and don't sign any documents without legal advice.

Chapter-30

Subprime Loans: You can Lose your Home

It is wrapped up in mystery and teems with trouble. But to the borrower, it is a panacea, a welcome relief at a second chance in life. Subprime loans have been on the increase in recent years and millions of unsuspecting borrowers have become its victims. A few weeks ago, the national media reported that many borrowers have lost their homes. What started originally as a trickle has now become an epidemic. The result has been that some of the biggest lenders have faced bankruptcy or the cutting back of staff.

New Century Financial was one of the biggest provider of mortgages to low income borrowers. It has since filed for bankruptcy and has stated that it will reduce its workforce by 54 per cent. The subprime fall-out has also hit other stalwarts in the banking sector such as HCBC. This bank was exposed to $11 billion worth of bad credit through its HFC household programs. What are subprime loans? How are unsuspecting buyers caught in the trap and what can be done to reform the mortgage industry to prevent innocent borrowers from losing their homes?

Is the dream of most persons to own a home and to live in relative comfort and security far-fetched? However, they may not meet the qualifications for a mortgage. In other words, they are credit risks. There is a range of descriptions that are used to classify a person as a credit risk. These include the late payment of loans, foreclosures, the re-possession of property or bankruptcy in the last five years. The credit risk category can also include someone with a high default probability. This normally means a credit bureau (FICO) score of below 660 points. When the ratio of debt owed to income is 50 per cent or greater, or the person does not have a cash flow based on bank statements, then that person is also deemed to be in a 'credit risk' category.

According to Consumer Reports, about 20 per cent of US consumers have credit scores of 620 or below. This is a high percentage when translated into actual borrowers. When 20 per cent of consumers are shut out from the traditional lending institutions the subprime lenders are not far away. The Federal Reserve Bulletin reports that minorities are most likely to take out subprime loans. The figures for 2005 show that 49 per cent of Blacks, 21 per cent of Whites and 33 per cent of Hispanics were borrowers of subprime loans.

Subprime borrowers live in poor and distressed neighborhoods, are less likely to have a college education and are susceptible to the fancy talk of the loan sharks. Anecdotal evidence points to the fact that many borrowers were only too happy to apply for loans to purchase their homes through subprime outlets. For example, in 2005, George Mason in the Bronx, New York, bought a house worth $200,000. He was offered a mortgage of $190,000 at a rate of eight per cent. The income of the Mason family was just enough to cover the mortgage and make ends meet.

Mason had a rude awakening in 2007 when the interest rate shot up by another two per cent. This meant that the Mason family would have to spend everything on the mortgage or risk losing their home. Mason is not alone. In the New York area, hundreds of families are affected in this way. In Mason's case, he was able to put down $10,000 on the mortgage. But what happens when the borrower has taken 100 per cent of the value of their home?

In cases where the full sum is borrowed against the property, the borrower must pray that the property value remain stable or does not decrease. When the latter happens, the borrower is 'under water' which means that he or she owes the lender more than the home is worth. There are two options that are presented to the borrower. The individual can either keep the payments or default. When borrowers default, there is a loss of revenue and the lender loses money. What is the impact of the subprime mortgage fiasco in Queens, New York? It is well known that in Queens, there is a large immigrant community.

According to one realtor, the subprime mortgage was good in the beginning for immigrants. A person could have obtained a mortgage with only five per cent down. Since the abuse of subprime occurred, foreclosures have become rampant and there have been "fake and fraudulent transactions". These fake buyers have taken away 50 per cent of the market in Queens, according to some realtors. How was this possible?

A house may be listed for $600,000 when the actual price is $500,000. When this happens, two factors may converge. The first is that the buyer may want the price that he or she thinks the house is worth, but it is the second that is open to abuse. It is known that there are persons who will make purchases by promising a seller whatever price is asked. Since they do not have any intention of living in the house, it can easily be 'flipped' for a profit.

The bottom has fallen out of subprime mortgages with foreclosures and default payments. The practice of buying up homes and selling them at a profit in minority communities has been exposed. In the circumstances, rental housing remains an option but the prospective buyer should be advised to tread cautiously when making the big leap to buy a house. It does a great deal of good to ask questions even if they appear repetitive and boring because it is the borrower who will be stuck with a lifetime of payments.

Chapter-31

The Car Bailout

The then CEO of General Motors, Rick Wagoner, tried to be dramatic in his appeal. He said, "This is much more than just Detroit. It is about saving the US economy from a catastrophic collapse." Mr Wagoner was addressing the Senate Banking Committee and with the heads of Chrysler and Ford. He was pleading for $25 billion to bail out the car industry. This bailout, he said, "would span the financial chasm that has opened before us". At the end of the Senate hearing, politicians told the Big Three to come up with a recovery plan if they want the $25 billion rescue. They had until 2 December 2008 to do so.

How did the car industry in the United States got to this point and why did they need a bailout? According to reports from the automobile industry, people do buy American cars. In 2007, General Motors outsold Toyota in the United States and abroad, but that is not all. Ford outsold Honda in the United States and Chrysler sold more cars and trucks in the United States than Nissan and Hyundai combined. As far as the foreign market is concerned, American-made cars are also riding the waves.

The world's second largest car market is China. General Motors is the top selling car-maker in China. One reason for the popularity of American cars is their fuel efficiency. General Motors is more fuel-efficient than Honda Accord, Honda Civic and Toyota Corolla. In an age of hybrid vehicles, Ford and General Motors again outscored Honda and Nissan. In 2011, the Chevy Volt will be the world's first all electric car. Incidentally, General Motors state that 20 of its models give more than 30 miles to the gallon.

In view of these positives, it is interesting to read the comments of the politicians on the local car industry. Senator Christopher Dodd (D-Conn) had stated, "This is not the first time that the leaders of the automobile industry have presented Congress with a doomsday scenario in connection with a cry for help." According to the Senator, "The industry is seeking treatment for wounds that are largely self-inflicted." Senator Charles Schumer (D-NY) had asked for reassurances that include the industry "wont come back again in six months in the same sinking boat, asking for another 50 billion dollars to plug more holes".

The begging bowl that was taken to Washington had to be seen in the context of the wider financial crisis that was affecting the United States. Hefty pay raises, big bonuses and bad judgment had crippled some of the big firms. Lehman Brothers was ruined. The insurance giant AIG had decided to forego bonuses as have UBS, Barclays and Goldman Sachs. The former head of AIG, Robert Willumstad, rejected a severance package of $22 million when he left in disgrace.

The federal government had decided to bail out Citigroup. It argued that Citigroup was too big to fall. Citigroup has two million accounts, branches in over 100 countries and is worth $2 trillion.

Then Treasury Secretary Henry Paulson informed the nation that the $750 billion package would not go toward helping Americans who face foreclosures. Instead, "it was intended to shore up the foundation of our economy by stabilizing the financial system."

A powerful argument in favor of a car industry bailout is that a normal chapter 11 Bankruptcy will not lead to a restructuring of the industry. Instead, it will lead to a Chapter 7 total liquidation and this in turn would cost millions of jobs to companies. During this period of economic woe, are General Motors, Ford and Chrysler too big to fail? The argument to help them is that thousands of suppliers and dealerships depend on the Big Three.

It is estimated that two million Americans work in the car industry while Wall Street firms hold millions of dollars in high interest debt. It is further suggested that a bailout package may actually facilitate a merger between GM and Chrysler. Some experts believe that once this merger takes place, a combined company would be able to cut billions of dollars in costs.

Despite these arguments, there are critics who feel that the big three have to be blamed for the situation. Professor William Watson who teaches economics at McGill University says that companies are not like banks. If people start withdrawing their money the banking system collapses, "but if GM falls, cars will still be bought and sold. GM's failure would be good for Toyota, not bad".

Joseph Stiglitz, winner of the Nobel Prize in economics, feels that "these companies ought to go bankrupt… That doesn't mean the company ceases to exist. What it means is that you restructure the finances." Professor Thomas Friedman shares a similar view. He says, "The US car industry's troubles are to be blamed on a very un-innovative business culture, visionless management and overly generous labor contracts."

Dana Perino, the then White House spokeswoman, had said that President Bush would be willing to release the money if the Big Three can show "viability and a willingness to make tough decisions to restructure themselves." Ms Perino had quickly corrected herself and said that this retrofit was actually a giveaway. She acknowledged that "there was virtually no way that the taxpayers would actually be paid back."

The Treasury Department says that another 800 billion would be needed to shore up the economy and get things moving again. Should some of this money go to bailout the car industry? But public opinion seems to be against it.

Chapter-32

Those Hefty Bonuses!

When Wall Street sneezes, the rest of the country catches a cold! In 2008, Wall Street bankers received $19 billion in bonuses. This prompted President Barack Obama to remark, "There will be time for bankers to make profits, and there will be time for them to get bonuses—now is not that time. This is the height of irresponsibility. It is shameful." During the economic crisis, one of the main criticisms has been the huge corporate payments that were given to top executives. It was felt that greed in the financial sector was a contributing factor to the economic stagnation that has hit much of the world.

According to President Obama, these were the same institutions that were "teetering on collapse". They were the ones that were also asking buyers to bail them out. As is well known, Congress passed a $700 billion bailout package. Another $819 billion stimulus package was passed to further help the economy. Public opinion in the United States and in other countries appear to be on the side of those who want to see the titanic bonuses curtailed. But there are dissenting voices and the former Mayor of New York, Rudy Giuliani, is one of them.

Giuliani has argued in favor of giving bonuses. He said on CNN, "If you somehow take the bonus out of the economy, it really will create unemployment. It means less spending in restaurants, less spending in department stores, so everything has an impact." Giuliani recalled that when he was Mayor of New York City, "one of the ways in which you determine New York City's budget tax revenue is Wall Street bonuses." In other words, New York City is kept afloat by these huge increases. The views of President Obama and Rudy Giuliani then appeared to be in stark opposition to each other.

In March 2009, in a Congressional hearing, the lawmakers in Washington were outraged when they heard that the American Insurance Group (AIG) was giving tens of millions of dollars in bonuses to employees. The Democrats in the House suggested that a 90 per cent tax be levied on these bonuses. Charles Rangel, the Chairman of the House Ways and Means Committee, stated that the high taxes were an attempt to stave off and reverse the damage that was caused by the greed of the financial system. It was revealed that AIG had received about $170 billion in government funds under the Troubled Asset Relief Program that was approved by Congress in 2008 to help certain financial institutions.

But some Congressmen have stated what many in the nation have felt for a long time. Democrat Paul Kanjorski said that the bonuses were outrageous at a time when millions of Americans are hurting. What was the response of AIG to this criticism? Edward Liddy, the CEO of AIG, said that the bonuses were legal contracts that had to be paid. The risks would be greater to the company and the economy if the bonuses were not paid. Liddy further added that employees in their financial products division who received $100,000 or more in bonuses have been asked to return "at least half the money". It is not clear how effective this has been so far, nor is it clear how the economy would be affected if the bonuses were not paid.

The Chairman of the House Financial Services Committee, Barney Frank, argues that the government should use the leverage it has as a majority holder in AIG to recover some of the funds. He said, "The time has come for the federal government to assert greater ownership rights." There are a number of strategies that have been proposed to handle excessive awards of bonuses to corporate employees. President Obama has suggested that a cap should be put in place that would limit the compensation for bank executives that take the bailout money at $500,000.

For many people who are struggling to make ends meet, a cap on bonuses may be a good thing. There are those who may think that $500,000 is still too excessive as a bonus. But what is the response of the Republicans to this idea? Senate Majority Whip Jon Kyl (R-AZ) said that is it not a good thing in America for a government to tell a company what it can pay to its employees? Senator Mel Martinez (R-FL) stated, "It's troubling to have a government telling shareholders how much they can pay executives."

There is also another powerful voice that is opposed to a cap or a ceiling. Senator James Inhofe (R-OK) said that while he is one of the chief defenders of Obama's bipartisanship, he is totally opposed to the idea of a cap. According to him, "As I was listening to Obama make these statements, I thought, is this still America? Do we really tell people how to run a business and who to pay and how much to pay?"

In an effort to answer this question, the *Economist* has a rather different view. It points out that the banking industry is committing political suicide by paying out large bonuses only a year after the government intervened to help it. During the last year, banking staff received four times as much as the shareholders. Bailing out the banks was not a bad idea, economists contend. It made sense to keep cash flowing to the wider economy and help banks rebuild their capital but did anyone really expect it to go to the employee? Fixing caps on a few employees appear to be more symbolic than punitive. It has, so far, lacked a sense of purpose and retrospective taxes doesn't appear to be a great idea either.

What then can work within the confines of the law? Governments can reclaim the subsidy given to banks working on the principle that banks are too big to fail. For example, if the top five investment banks were to pay a little over two per cent on "uninsured borrowing" the *Economist* estimates that the subsidy could be reduced from 120 billion per year to 36 billion. The grant of hefty bonuses would have to be reduced in the face of accountability by the banks. But for this to happen, banks will have to be willing to support it. Given the statements from Washington and elsewhere, self-regulation is a rather distant goal.

The re-election of Michael Bloomberg as Mayor of New York is certain to have an impact on Wall Street. It will be looking for stability while the City will want accountability. It is interesting to note that during the Mayoral campaign, the economy did not feature much in the debates. However, in the third term of the Bloomberg administration, the economic status of the City will definitely be a factor in policy and Wall Street will figure prominently in it.

Section-VI

Social and Cultural Issues

Chapter-33

Where have the Fathers gone?

Fathers. Where have they gone? A 1996 Gallup poll states, "Seventy-nine per cent of Americans feel that the most significant family or social problem facing America is the physical absence of the father from the home." As another Father's Day came and went, there is the realization that fatherhood is fragile. Finding fathers in some families is turning out to be a harrowing experience. As is usual with issues of this kind, generalizations ought to be qualified. Many households have fathers who are kind, loving, hardworking and dependable. They fit the role to a hilt and these fathers should be hailed as excellent role models. But what about fathers who neglect and abandon their children, who display anger and cruelty and who even when they are around treat their families with disrespect? A house without a good father is robbed of nurturing and sustained care and involvement. Father's Day should be replaced with 'Responsible Father's Day'.

In today's society, divorce rates are extremely high. It is estimated that of every 100 marriages, 50 will end in divorce. This results in children being caught in an emotional tug-of-war, of ex-spouses using children as revenge for past actions and of children growing up and feeling insecure. Research has shown that structural factors such as unemployment and drug use and crime have hindered fathers from fulfilling their duties.

Salim Muwakkil in 2005 examined the reasons as to why black men are missing from their families. He found that "the overwhelming absence of black men has always been one of the most depressing facts about life in America's public housing developments." He cites the case of the Chicago Housing Authority where women are the vast majority of lease-holders, and men are like ghosts in the projects. The statistics across the nation are troublesome and may help to explain why a good many fathers in the black community are not around.

Jonathan Tilove, writing in the New Jersey *Star Ledger,* states that for the city of East Orange, there are 37 more adult women than men. What has accounted for this disparity? Tilove states that most of the missing men are dead or are in the military or are in prison. The author concludes that the gender imbalance is a snapshot of what is troubling America today. In the United States, it is estimated that adult black women outnumber adult black men by two million. According to the Census Bureau, this gap represents 26 per cent while for the white population it is only 8 per cent.

The gender gap affects all nationalities. Middle-class women are increasing among blacks and whites. This means that the more educated a woman becomes, the less likely it is that she will have a big family. Progress among women is welcome news but as women advance, men are falling behind. Many young men are in prison because of drug related and other offenses. When poverty increases, the streets begin to take over.

Schools are neglected and assumptions about the academic talents of youngsters are made early in the school system. The cycle becomes vicious. Young boys are alienated from the school system and they turn to the streets for diversions. Drop out rates increase and the uneducated youth becomes the fodder for prison. A recent study has found that since 1995, only 38 per cent of young men have graduated in the inner cities of Chicago.

What security can this growing population of unmarketable men give to a wife and children? Many young men become the victims of homicide. In fact, homicide is the leading cause of death among young men, regardless of race and color. Michael Gurion, a former college lecturer in Washington, stated that in the 1990s, there were more young women in his classes than men. The women were also getting better grades. He pointed out, "The young men didn't care much what I taught: literature, writing and psychology. They were bright kids but their faces said that sitting and listening were not really about what they were and wanted."

In 2005, Gurion interviewed an administrator at Howard University who revealed one of the biggest problems at Howard. According to the administrator, "We are having problems recruiting and retaining male students. We are about a two to one ratio, women to men." Apparently, Howard University is not alone. All across America colleges and Universities are grappling with the case of the mysteriously vanishing male. Gurion concludes, "If we don't reverse the downward trend soon, we will gradually diminish the male identity, and thus the productivity and the mission of the next generation of young men and all the ones that follow."

Education is a crucial determinant for social ability. There are successful images of men who have made it to the top. Bill Gates, Warren Buffett, and Barack Obama come to mind. But there are also young men who, without a proper education, work in lower level jobs. Then there are those who waste away their lives on drugs and gambling. They play video games endlessly and the world passes them along the way. Gone are the days when the maxim "the men will get a job and provide" used to be true.

Arguably, not every young man has to go to college to succeed or to be a good husband. While this is true, there can be no doubt that a college degree opens doors. Recent trends suggest that a bleak future lies ahead for those who do not possess a college education. Sociologists contend that, "a young man who does not finish school or go to college will earn less than half of what a college graduate earns. He will be three times more likely to be unemployed and homeless. He will be more likely to develop substance abuse problems, get divorced and engage in violence against women."

In addition, some researchers found that this population will pay less into social security, depend on government welfare, abandon their children and fail to pay child support. This is a damning indictment on a young population that does not try hard enough. It also explains why young men fail to take life and responsibilities seriously. Where have the fathers gone? Diann Thompson, an executive director of the America Coalition for Fathers and Children, believes that the answer lies in America's judicial system.

Ms Thompson argues that women receive custodial rights in 81 per cent of the time. According to the coalition, "Nothing stuns a divorced father as deeply as hearing a judge relegate him from a caring role-model to a visitor in his children's lives. More important, no child should ever lose a parent as a result of a divorce in which he or she had no choice."

The Coalition of Fathers and Children provided statistics that are alarming. For instance, fatherless children are twice as likely to drop out of school. What is even more revealing is the cycle of despair that follows the break up of families. Joan Berlin Kelly and Judith Wallerstein in their book, *Surviving the Break Up,* point out that more than half of mothers report that their children should have little or no role with fathers following a divorce. The vanishing male is also a fact of life in the Indo-Caribbean community in New York as well, where a significant number of young men abandon their children.

What are some of the effects of a fatherless home? Researchers conclude that children are twice as likely to drop out of school and that over 70 per cent of children who are in juvenile detention come from fatherless homes. Girls are 164 per cent likely to become pregnant and 900 per cent more likely to suffer from sexual abuse with no father in the home. Given the state of fatherhood in our society, what can be done to get fathers to stay at home and be more responsible? Obviously, it would be ideal if there were no divorces and every family can live happily ever after. But we do not live in a perfect world and break-ups will happen.

There is no one solution that will fit all the problems. The most appropriate solution would be to start a marriage on the right footing. This means that great care and thought should go into areas such as compatibility before marriage plans are made. A healthy respect between husband and wife and for their families is also a pre-requirement. The relationship, after marriage, may be strained at times but constant dialogue between partners can be helpful. The adage that a husband and wife should never go to bed angry at each other applies. It may seem old-fashioned to some but a relationship that is built with God at the center will last all tribulations.

Responsible fathers would not neglect their children. The day of the deadbeat father should be outlawed. Fathers should pay up and take an active role in their child's life. It is heartening to note that certain colleges are now striving to attract more male students. This may not magically transform families but it will lay the groundwork for a group of educated men who can be leaders and change our outlook on marriage and relationships. The last thing we need is another wave of non-resident fathers.

Chapter-34

Shopping Frenzy Can Kill

For many, the holiday season is the best time of the year. There are reunions, parties, and black cake and ginger beer. Then there are the sales in which people's minds are centered on one thing only: they have to be the first in line to snap up the bargains. In England and other parts of Europe, 26 December or Boxing Day is when the big sales are offered. People would wait in the freezing cold for days to make the mad rush to buy that fur coat at Selfridges or Harrods. A few years ago, New Year's day sales were introduced in some countries and the result has been the same.

There is a stampede, a human bullfight to get to a particular item. In the United States, there are no Boxing Day sales but there is Black Friday, the day after Thanksgiving. All the talk of recession seemed to have made little impact as thousands camped outside the major outlets to walk away with marked down loot. But before the doors are thrust open, it is important to pause and take stock of where we are heading and why American consumers find themselves looking for artificial bargains.

The most telling observation is that people have been conditioned into believing that the holiday season is a time to spend. But lavish consumption in December can lead to penny pinching or downright starvation for some in January. Who cares, once the flat screen televisions are acquired for a hundred dollars less.

American businesses along with slick and sophisticated marketing can create shortages and anxiety. These propel people to join long lines to buy things that they do not really need. It is a ploy that the communists have used so well to keep people "in line" during the heyday of socialism. In the United States, it does not matter whether we are pumping money into the economies of China, Taiwan or Japan; the clothes and gadgets are all that matter. If there is no cash, then plastic will do!

The reality is that millions of Americans owe banks more money than the value of their homes. This makes additional borrowing difficult, if not impossible. Banks are having a hard time keeping above water. The message for American consumers is to save the extra dollar and to live within their means. In a good many cases, working hours have been cut and employees have lost their jobs. It is against this background that a "bizarre homicide" took place in Valley Stream, New York.

On the morning of Black Friday, Jdimytai Damour went to work at Wal Mart. Around 4:55 in the morning, the doors were opened and the throng pushed forward. In minutes, there was a mad stampede and Damour was trampled by a fanatic mob bent on grabbing clothes, electronics and televisions. According to a *Daily News* editorial, "managers were plainly aiming to start the Christmas shopping season with a bang by offering deep discounts keyed to a 5 am opening. They provided lots of reasons for a big and excited crowd to gather in the early morning darkness, but not the means to keep it from morphing into a mob." The *Daily News* went on to make this poignant observation: "When you pump up the volume of crowds with doorbuster sales and early openings, you must shoulder the responsibility for the safety of customers and staff." What the editorial did not say is that the media was also responsible for the sales hype through its advertisements and coverage. Where in the media were there warnings of safety prior to the sales? The media is an accessory to a tragedy that could have been prevented if someone had taken the job of warning people to be on their best behavior.

In the days leading up to the sales, there were articles in newspapers and reports on various television shows about the big sales on Black Friday. It is evident that what happened has now backfired on the media. Apart from the Wal-Mart tragedy in Valley Stream, shopping frenzy in other parts of the country has also led to violence. In Michigan, shoppers fought over merchandise. In California, two men shot each other in a mall and both died. In New York, a pregnant woman was trampled at another Wal-Mart, and at another store, a woman tripped and fell and lost her wig!

At a Best Buy store, there was "a mob scene to get bargain-priced laptops and other electronics." What is remarkable and defies explanation is that shoppers went about their business in many of these cases without the slightest regard for the injured. The death of Damour and the violence of other stores have brought into question the nature of our society. Some writers point out that in 1996, throngs of shoppers mobbed stores for the "Tickle me Elmo". The store in question was Wal-Mart and a clerk was knocked unconscious by a surge of 300 shoppers.

It is apparent that we have learned little from the previous bouts of insane shopping. According to one lady from Baldwin City in Kansas, "Most of the time, it was not like we were looking for anything in particular; we were just looking." In Georgia, financial psychologist Mary Gresham said that there are two primary reasons for the Black Friday phenomenon. "The first," she says, "is that it has become a ritual. The second is what we call the psychology of the herd. Because everyone else is up and doing it, suddenly you feel a strong sense to do it too. Its very euphoric when you are in it." One should try explaining this euphoric feeling to the family of Jdimytai Damour, the young man who was trampled to death at Wal-Mart.

The tragedy of Damour and others is really that of materialism and accumulation. The big sales do not really satisfy any need except a hunger for accumulation, argue some commentators. They point out that we live in an age of materialism and a culture of greed. As Black Friday gives way to Christmas Day, let us remember that the greatest gift is not to be found in a mall. It begins in the heart. There is no price for compassion care and love.

Chapter-35

Are the Children Listening?

Are the children listening? Many parents complain that they are tired of saying the same things over and over to their children. It's like throwing water on a withered plant. Since there are two sides to the question that was posed, it should be stated at the outset that many children do listen to their parents and teachers, and should be commended for their efforts. But there are those who do not listen, who feel that they know it all and who bear the scars to prove it. This article is addressed to that population with the hope that some good can come out of a change of behavior.

Children these days live in a fast lane. They grow up in a hurry and want to see and experience life quickly. Reality is here and now and it has to be seen to be believed. This can and does lead to a life of complications. A girl from a well-to-do family is allowed to go on a date at the age of 11. The following week, she breaks up with her boyfriend and goes on another date with someone else. This is a far cry from growing up in Guyana or elsewhere in the Caribbean. What do the parents know about 'dating'? But take the case of Clive and his family.

Clive migrated from Guyana to America in the 80s. He settled in Georgia with his three young sons. As he watched them grow, he kept telling his boys about the importance of truth, honesty and hard work. When Clive opened a business in Atlanta, the boys had to make weekly trips to New York to buy produce in order to stock the store. Twenty years later, the family can be considered a success. What has led to their success in America? One of the boys explains, "When we came to America, we had nothing at all. But we were determined to do well. We listened to our parents. If they told us not to be out at certain time, we listened. There are times when we might get upset but we knew it was for our own good. In addition, we never took any major decisions without first informing our parents and getting their approval."

In another example, two friends grew up in the same neighborhood. They shared the same cultural background and went to the same school but one was obedient to her parents and hardly got into any trouble. Her friend, on the other hand, was rebellious. She did not listen to her parents and did what she wanted. What was the reason for her behavior? She explains that it was largely due to peer pressure. She had to behave in a certain way to conform or else the group would ostracize her.

Peer pressure is one of the main reasons why people disregard parental advice. In the immigrant community, conflicting values are always vying for attention, and in many cases, it is those who are associated with the "in group" that win in the end. For example, immigrant parents were raised in the Caribbean, or elsewhere, to respect the rights of others, to save for a rainy day and to value education. It is a fact that a good percentage of children in North America do the opposite. The values of parents are in competition with those of friends in the schools and in the streets.

The use of profanities or curses, the 'N-word' and disrespecting elders and women are quite common in the school-age population. So too is the use of drugs and the joining of gangs. Drug use among teenagers and adolescents has reached an all time high in New York City, according to many educators. Drugs are such an insidious poison that they leave young persons unable to cope with the realities and pressures around them. Children who are "high" are listless and cannot function in schools. They end up flunking their classes, and by the time they come to their senses, it is usually too late. Peer pressure is again another reason for drug use and for children to disregard the advice of their parents.

The family is the agent for social, cultural and political development of the child. According to some psychologists, "A stable and loving family plays many roles in our lives, but the foundation is one of unconditional acceptance, demonstrated by attentive listening. Parents have been listening to each other since the beginning of time." The sad fact is that due to many pressures in society such as unemployment, lack of housing and security and welfare, many families are on the brink of breaking up and children are caught in the middle. Listening and communication skills are thus sacrificed at the expense of frustration and anger. While it is true that "an increased emphasis on listening will help families practice more and honest communication," pent up feelings can also be destructive.

The use of technology has made communication easier. In the old days, a child would leave home to play with his friends and it was difficult for parents to make contact. But thanks to today's technology, parents and children can keep in contact with children with a touch of a button. But does this really happen? There are parents who complain that mobile or cell phones do not mean that the child will pick up when a call is made from home.

One exasperated parent states, "I bought a phone for my son. But whenever I call him, the voicemail comes on; he seldom answers the phone. What is the point? However, when he comes home and his friends call him, he is quick to answer." For another parent, it's because the children have it too good that they are not listening to or following directions. How many times they tell you that they will be home by a certain hour and they are not? It's always about their friends. They seem to have more time for their friends, she said.

In reinforcing the importance of listening, Dr Pranela Rameshwar, a Guyanese scientist at New Jersey School of Medicine, makes a most interesting point. She states that on a rainy day in Guyana, a teacher took her class and gave the students a pep talk. What came out of that talk is that if students listen, they will learn. Dr Rameshwar said that that was the turning point in her life. That simple message about listening changed her life. She is today one of the leading scientists in the world in stem cell research. The first thing she tells her students is that listening is one of the most important tools in learning.

Chapter-36

Don Imus: Nappy and Happy?

It was supposed to be a moment of unalloyed joy, a pure feeling of triumph. The women's basketball team of Rutgers University had scaled a collective mountain. They came close to winning the championship and in the process make many people proud. Then came Don Imus and his entourage. They made a living by poking fun at others. The morning of his simulcast was like any other. When it came to the main event, he praised the beauty of the white Tennessee team that had conquered the young ladies of Rutgers. For Imus, the Rutgers women were "nappy-head hos, I'll tell you that."

A translation is in order. The term 'nappy-head' is not a person bedecked with flowers or fragrance. In fact, the term has connotations that are loaded with insults and historical umbrage. The word 'nappy' is a slang for someone who is dirty and unkempt. It relates specifically to African-American hair. Some years ago, a black writer, Carolivia Herron, wrote a children's book with the words "nappy hair" as part of the title. There was an uproar among some scholars. In short, it does not matter who uses the term; it is objectionable. The term 'ho' is a vulgar reference for someone who sells her body for money.

Don Imus, in an effort to have some fun, referred to the Rutgers basketball team in these now infamous words. This was not the only time that Imus has delved into indiscretions. They were hardly funny. In his decades in the media, Don Imus, the shock-jock, has made fun of many people and has insulted their nationalities. Some years ago, the *New York Times* assigned a black correspondent, Gwen Ifill, to cover the White House. Imus commented, "Isn't it wonderful that the *New York Times* lets the cleaning lady cover the White House?"

This was an affront to scholarship, to ethnicity, and to all people of color. It may have drawn a few laughs but it derided talent and hard work. Imus ranted later that Hovic Kurtz, a columnist for the *Washington Post* was a " beanie wearing Jewboy". The Arabs too incurred his wrath. He would routinely describe them as "towel-heads". His writing team laughed their heads off and the coffers of his employers swelled into millions. The elite flocked to his show. They reveled in the big audience: the cutting edge of a liturgy in which a person's power in the media can raise millions for charity and propel a book to the top slot.

But in the Rutgers case, Imus went too far. The past has a way of catching up with indiscretions. The money tree of CBS and MSNBC had to go. His remarks were toxic. They hit a raw nerve but arguably it was the age of technology that brought him to boot. In the days of radio, his remarks may have drifted into thin air and became lost into the cacophony of race and class wars. There would have been complaints but the difference in this case is that the Imus show was simulcast.

It could be downloaded and placed on various websites. On 6 April, two days after his remarks, the storm of protests had grown substantially. Millions had seen the 51 second clip and there was pressure from various groups to take action. The advertisers started to pull out. This was followed by a statement from MSNBC that it was removing Imus from his regular schedule.

Leslie Moonves, chairman of CBS, met with Reverends Al Sharpton and Jesse Jackson and CBS responded by firing Imus. This happened before Imus met with the women's basketball team. The meeting was described as "productive" by Rutgers coach C Vivian Stringer. What are the lessons that can be learned from the Imus incident?

The most obvious is that freedom of expression is guaranteed by the laws. However, John Stuart Mills' dictum that unbridled speech can cause damage is still valid. Imus admitted that his remarks were hurtful and offensive. There is a line which when crossed can cause pain. The other lesson is that racism is alive in America, despite our attempts to wish it away. The action of MSNBC and CBS is commendable. They distanced themselves from the stereotypes. But there are other deeper implications that can be highlighted.

Those who support Don Imus have argued that his remarks should not be taken out of context. They pointed out that what Imus said is nothing that is not reported on a daily basis in rap, and hip-hop songs. In other words, black entertainers can refer to women of their community in the vilest way possible, without any sanctions. These so-called artists sell millions by using women as targets for their abuse and yet no one can impose any restrictions on them.

For example, what penalty was imposed on Jay-Z, Ludacris, and

Snoop Dogg when they used words such as "ho" and "bitch" in their songs? Jay-Z has uttered the "N" word in his songs on numerous occasions without any consequences. What is the impact of this on the young? Many young people who buy their CDs have mixed feelings about a ban on suggestive lyrics in songs. A group of eighth grade students in a Queens public school stated that banning the offensive lyrics would be counter-productive. They point out that if the vulgar expressions were banned, the artists will still record them, and sell them "underground".

But there are other unresolved issues. Don Cheadle, who acted elegantly in *Hotel Rwanda* has argued that the N word is reflective of the black experience. He sees nothing wrong in its use. Many black students will argue that when the N word ends with an "r", it is to be outlawed. However, when it ends with an "a", that's acceptable, but only if used by blacks.

This argument is confusing. The use of the N word under any circumstances should be outlawed. What about hos and bitches and curse words? These words too have no place in any form of conversations. Reverend Al Sharpton has promised that at his National Action Network, dubbed the Hip Hop Summit, he will outlaw the use of vulgar lyrics in songs. The videos that accompany them must also be banned from the airwaves. We live in a culture in which women are mistreated and disrespected all too easily. Reverend Kerry Rogers points out that the N word is synonymous with over 400 years of pain and a struggle for identity. There is then a responsibility for all to respect each other and to practice tolerance, according to Reverend Rogers.

Don Imus has had his day on popular radio. He may come back, given the role of money in our culture. However, at least in one celebrated case, the shock-jock found that his audience was unafraid to stand up for dignity and self-respect.

Chapter-37

Social Networking

When John McCain said that he did not know how to send an e-mail, his campaign lost its technological shine. Barack Obama, on the other hand, couldn't imagine life without his Blackberry. He took every opportunity to show his finesse with computers and the world of social networking. Scholars have argued that the recent Presidential campaign was perhaps the most technologically advanced in living memory. One would recall that important announcements by Obama were made on smart phones. The history of social networking shows that there are vistas yet to be opened. In 1997, '6degrees.com' was the first and only site that was devoted to social networking. The following year drew a blank.

The future of social networking was in doubt even though three other sites opened up in 1999. '6degrees' incidentally folded up in the year 2000. By 2003, there were 13 sites devoted to social networking and a brave new world had opened up with infinite possibilities. The founding of Google added a revolution to it, and by 2005, there were Yahoo, Youtube and Facebook. Today, these sites together with Myspace, Friendster, and Linkedin are ruling the roost. There is an explosion of information on the superhighway and woe be to those who do not know how to use a mouse.

Social networking has become popular as a result of the internet. But long before Bill Gates, scholars have been working in the field of social science and have explored the complex sets of relationships from interpersonal to international. As early as 1954, social networking encompassed the whole to the part and from the behavior to attitude. According to one view, "Social network analysis produces an alternate view. Naming the attributes of individuals are less important than their relationships and ties with other actors within the network." The conclusion from the studies of anthropologists is that social networks are so powerful that they play a key role in the success of the group.

In the corporate world, social networks can be instrumental in price fixing, limiting competition and acquiring information. The point is that at what level is the individual at the center of all these many relationships? One of the key findings in social networking is that the chain of relationships that connect people are not extended as some may think. For example, the psychologist Stanley Milgram found that people can trace their relationships through five intermediaries. This led to "six degrees of separation" theory. How is all of this relevant to the internet? An experiment at Columbia University found "that about five to seven degrees of separation are sufficient for connecting people through e-mail.

These conclusions arguably form the body of theory that was used to devise the powerful engines of the internet. We have reached a point where millions of subscribers do little else but sit at their computers and update various pages and websites. One recent study in the Journal *Communication in Society* stated, "What makes social networking sites unique is not that they allow individuals to meet strangers, but rather that they enable users to articulate and make visible the social networks. The public display of connections is a crucial component of social networking."

In February 2010, Facebook celebrated its sixth birthday. A year is indeed a long time in cyberworld. But the popularity of Facebook is matched only by Google. As is well known, Facebook is the largest social network online and with 350 million users, only India and China have more people. The information showed on Facebook is staggering. Everyday the users post about 60 million updates and about 4 billion bits of information is shared worldwide. Nearly 70 per cent of the subscribers of Facebook live outside of the United States. This shows the growing power of the technology abroad. There is little doubt that social networking has improved communications in leaps and bounds. But they have gone much further. They have crossed barriers and have brought exclusives that hitherto might never be known.

A number of examples come to mind. In the Mumbai tragedy, the world relied on Twitter for updates and live pictures of what was happening on the ground. These reports were carried live on CNN and on other networks. Last year, when the demonstrations occurred in Iran to protest the outcome of the elections, it was Twitter again, followed by other channels that broke the stories and showed footage of other events. The earthquake in Chile in late February 2010 was reported around the world with speed and amazing pictures. The Facebook site brought many families together and carried appeals for help.

Surfing the net, particularly the social networking sites, can be a time consuming task. Australia heads the list with those who spend hours on these sites. The users in Australia spend nearly eight hours a day networking while in Britain this figure is seven hours and in the United States it is six hours. One of the main factors that can affect the growth of social networking is that of privacy. There is a popular saying that there is no delete button on the internet and this to a large extent is true. There are millions of pieces of information about people, including pictures, and not all are palatable. Sharing information is at the heart of social networking but if no effective controls exist and there is a free for all, the effects can be damaging.

There are cases of people who post information about themselves only to have it being seen by the world, without permission being given. Employers who interview prospective candidates could view the profiles online and may very well find information that put the candidates in a poor light. In February 2010, a senior officer of Facebook told an audience in California that "social norms had shifted and people had become more willing to share information about themselves more widely." The basis for this conclusion is not clear. Is it a case that these sites are making their own determination without the backing of hard scientific evidence?

It must be pointed out that in the end, social networking is big business. It offers a tremendous gateway for goods and services to be advertised worldwide. The data that people provide about themselves is used as advertisement purposes. What will the future of social networking look like given the ongoing innovation that is occurring? If you are in a store buying a box of corn flakes, you can send a picture of it to your mom's online page and she may tell you to buy a few boxes more. This is based on the assumption that the store has a keypad to transmit that data. But this need not be the case. The inventors seem to think that the biggest potential lies in the use of smart or mobile phones. Imagine using a phone to apply a multitude of applications that can track and transmit information in seconds. This appears to be the next wave.

The current technology is continuing to surprise. It has changed the world in several ways. When the internet was first invented, skeptics thought that it might fade as people may use it just to play games. However, the internet has led to a revolution and has produced such giants as Google and Amazon. Shopping online and receiving your purchases next day can be convenient as well as fun. In April 2010, Apple launched its own model of the future in the iPad and this too has taken the revolution to the next step.

Section-VII

Women and Children

Chapter-38

Don't Cheat on Your Wife!

It's awfully difficult being a politician these days. If you happen to be a Governor, things can get really messy. The news of politicians cheating on their wives fill pages in the newspapers. In many cases, the ever-suffering wives would stand next to the cheater and try to look composed as the Governor, Mayor or Senator grimaces, cries and repents for his so-called mistakes. Recently, Eliot Spitzer was thc golden boy of New York politics. He had won the race for Governor with a big majority. Then came a scandal. Spitzer had squired a mistress, had taken elaborate steps to hide it and was forced to resign as a result. As he tried to explain himself, his wife Silda looked at him as if she had drunk from a poison chalice.

Spitzer was replaced by David Paterson. Two days after he took the oath of office, we were in for a shock. Paterson informed the world that he too was unfaithful to his wife. But his wife wasn't prepared to take a backseat. She revealed that she had affairs as well. Who can forget Mayor Rudy Giuliani whose "very good friend" Judith Nathan became his wife. There is nothing wrong with that but Giuliani told the world that he was separating from his wife, Donna Hanover, before telling her himself.

Governor Jim McGreevey of New Jersey had no such qualms. He carried on a torrid affair with another man while he was married to his wife. As usual, the wife was the last person to know. In his autobiography, McGreevey explains that the kind of love he made was "boastful, whispering, and passionate". He was not talking about his wife. But even before Spitzer, Paterson, Giuliani and McGreevey, there was our fighter for Civil Rights, Jesse Jackson. It came as a surprise to most people when Jesse stood tearfully on the podium and told us all, "I have sinned." Jesse revealed that he had fathered a child outside of his marriage. The mother turned out to be a member of the staff.

It is apt to note that when a certain politician in the White House had problems of his own, it was Jesse Jackson who went and ministered to him. This politician was the ex-Governor of Arkansas, who later became President of the United States. It was President Bill Clinton who famously said, " I did not have sexual relations with that woman, Miss Lewinsky. I never told anybody to lie, not a single time; never." Well, we know differently now. When Bill Clinton was having his problems, a politician from South Carolina was calling for a new morality in the United States. He was fed up with the loose morals at the time and he wanted to see politicians being accountable and good family persons. This scion of virtue was none other than Mark Sanford. What about Senator John Edwards who admitted to an affair with Rielle Hunter, a member of his staff? He squandered his chances to run for high office and begged the public not "to beat up on him".

Recently, the media has had a field day with the exploits of Mark Sanford, the Governor of South Carolina. Sanford, in a series of poems and statements in the media, stated that he had crossed lines many times but he had crossed the sex line only once. It turns out that the line was with Maria Belen Chapur. She is a former TV journalist in Argentina who has the Governor switching planes, telling lies to his wife and his staff and using several hotels for meetings, including a few in New York. Maria is described as "attractive and athletic". This liaison may cost Sanford a run for the 2012 Presidency. He was only censured by the GOP in South Carolina. Where are Republican values when they are needed? These questions are far from Sanford's mind as he confesses that Maria is his "soul mate" while he tries to reconcile with his wife.

Why do men cheat on their wives? How can you know if your spouse is a cheater and what can be done to remedy the situation? The answer to the first question is rather complex. In a number of research studies, 92 per cent of men said that they cheated on their wives for reasons other than sex. The main reason why they cheated was because they felt under-appreciated. They did not get thoughtful attention from their wives and this led to insecurity. According to one study, "If somebody else, another woman is willing to make him feel good about himself, make him feel appreciated, admired and valuable, make him feel that he is the best person in the world, there is the risk that man will start a relationship with this other woman." The picture we usually get is that men are strong and lacking in emotions. The fact is that men are very emotional beings. It is estimated that only seven per cent of husbands tell their wives that they are having an affair, before being caught.

The main reason why men cheat on their wives has been attributed to emotional distance. It is suggested that one way to bridge this distance is to learn to appreciate husbands for the little things they do. For instance, if the husband is trying to prepare dinner but burns the food in the process, a good wife would praise him and appreciate his effort. In this way, everybody wins but what if this doesn't work and the husband cheats anyway? What should the wife do? Some psychologists argue that high-tech equipment is not needed to catch a cheating husband nor is a private investigator necessary.

If a wife really knows her husband, then she can tell if he's cheating on her. He will leave the clues. This means that all the wife has to do is put the pieces together. She needs to look at his behavior and also to find out if there are changes in his routine. If she knows from the outset then the two of them could work it out with the help of counselors, or therapists. But what if the husband is always cheating? Is there a way for him to stop? Several suggestions have been put forward to help the cheating husband. For instance, he should pause and think and evaluate the reasons as to why he's cheating.

The husband should use common sense and stay away from situations that may prove tempting, whether its chatting on the internet or going to bars. If nothing works and he is still cheating, then there are two courses that are open. He can either confess to the affair or face the possibility that his wife will eventually find out. If she asks for a separation or divorce, then her wishes should be respected. If children and property are involved, it becomes more complicated.

In the end of course, the cheating husband will have to deal with the question, "was it worth it?" Was it worth leaving his family to pursue another relationship on the side? There are those who will answer in the affirmative but in the majority of cases, extra-marital affairs end up in acrimony and ill-will and no one really wins. One thing is certain and that is a cheater must be prepared to live a life of lies and deceit and to invest a lot of time and energy and money in the relationship.

One former serial cheater has lamented his ways as a social butterfly. He has advice for all cheating husbands. For him, it's a question of options. Why break up a relationship that in many cases can be saved through communication and understanding? He appeals to all men to "think before you act. Use your head… wisely".

Chapter-39

The Pink Gang

They are like stars on a dark night. In one of India's poorest regions, a group of women are making the headlines. They wear pink saris and attack corruption with sticks and a no-nonsense attitude. They are the '*gulabi* gang' or the Pink Gang. In what many see as a revolution in the making, the Pink Gang take on the political establishment but its antipathy also extend to non-government organizations (NGOs). The Pink Gang believes that political parties and NGOs are part of the problem. According to their leader Sampat Devi, "politicians are always looking for kickbacks when they offer to fund us."

The Pink Gang has been around for only three years but they have already made an impact in the neighborhood. Donned in flowing pink saris, they have "trashed men who have beaten or abandoned their wives and unearthed corruption in the distribution of grain to the poor." What is the reason for the formation of the Pink Gang? Their leader explains that in Banda, Uttar Pradesh, help for the poor is almost non-existent. Corruption is the order of the day. The establishment is anti-poor. The idea is to heap shame on the wrongdoers so that they can do what is proper.

It is appropriate that Banda should be one of the places for the

Pink Gang to take root. Banda has been classified as one of the poorest districts in India. It has a population of over two million persons. The residents of Banda live in about 700 villages and belong to various castes, including the untouchables. In recent years, nature in the form of droughts, combined with poverty, have had a devastating impact on life in Banda. As is common in many parts of India and the Third World, women face the brunt of hardships in male-dominated societies. The activities of the Pink Gang have to be seen against a background of female suffering and this has made its impact all the more impressive and commendable.

Some scholars have argued that the problems affecting women in India are so powerful that it makes the fight tougher at every step. If one looks at sex determination and selection, it becomes evident that females have a difficult time. Deepali Gaur Singh, a political commentator, writes, "If there was ever a fight that appeared doomed from the start, then the battle against sex selective abortions in India would be the one topping the list." The sex determination kits are sold and resold in poor villages so that the sex of the child can be told in a matter of hours. In a society where boys are preferred, what happens to the female fetus? Laws are on the books banning selective abortions but how effective are they?

According to the *Hindustan Times,* gender testing and selection kits manufactured in the United States and Canada have now flooded Punjab. This state has one of the lowest sex ratios in India (874 females per 1000 males according to the 2001 Census). Dr Anurag Goswami of the Punjab Medical Council states, "Doctors who had been carrying out sex-determination tests through ultra sounds are now buying kits online and selling them."

Rampant poverty, discrimination, selective abortions and natural calamities have conspired to create difficult living conditions for people. As we have seen, those in the forefront of the struggle have to feed their families, using every mechanism at their disposal. It was like a breath of fresh air then when a group of women in pink saris decided to take matters in their own hands.

This group of women decided that they would no longer be subjected to corruption from officials in high places, and to husbands who shirk their duties and desert their families. The Pink Gang has been besieged with all kinds of problems to solve since its formation.

They include dowry deaths, child marriages, the shortage of water in village communities and how to deal with government agencies that steal money from the public. Recently, a woman brought her daughter who was thrown out of her home because her husband wanted Rs 20,000 from the girl's parents. This prompted the Pink Gang to act.

Sampat Devi assembled her gang and marched to the girl's house for an explanation from her husband. He was ordered to take her back and treat her well. The Pink Gang is quick to point out that it is not anti-men; rather it is anti-corruption. Many of its members have themselves suffered abuse and want it to end. Sampat Devi, its leader, was sold into marriage when she was nine-year old. She became a mother at 13 but what drove her to form the gang was the cruelty meted out to her sister. An alcoholic husband had dragged her sister by her hair in a courtyard. Sampat vowed that she had had enough.

She organized all the women and chased the erring husband in a cane field and gave him a public whipping.

Sampat Devi's bravery has drawn inevitable comparisons with that other Devi who took India into the headlines. Phoolan Devi was also from Uttar Pradesh. At 11, she was married to a widower 20 years her senior. She was abandoned shortly after marriage and was adopted by dacoits in the 1970s. As the story goes, Phoolan Devi escaped from her captors. She formed her own gang and after much violence, she surrendered.

In 1996, Phoolan Devi ran for a seat in the Indian Parliament as a Samajwadi candidate. She won the seat, lost it and won it again. This catapulted her to fame. But it was short-lived. Phoolan Devi was assassinated in July 2001. The years may have passed but even today the name of Phoolan Devi conjures up memories of a mythic figure. Sampat Devi (no relation) is confident that her Pink Gang can create more awareness to shame the officials to redress the wrongs done to women and to prevent new ones from happening.

What is the future of the Pink Gang? In the two years of its existence, the Gang has wrought important changes from the local administration. It has ruffled feathers beyond Banda. It is reported that in other communities, women are watching closely and may form themselves into groups to bring about similar changes. Sampat Devi has herself dabbled with local politics. She contested the state polls as an independent candidate but she lost, managing only 2,800 votes. Nevertheless, this was a big step for women in Banda. What is of even more importance is the need to use to Pink Gang to change attitudes in Banda.

The dalits or untouchables in Banda make up over 20 per cent of the population of the area. The daily wage for men is around Rs 40 while for women it is much lower. A recent survey found that lower caste students and staff face discrimination in employment. Dalit students are prevented from eating meals with higher caste students. What all this means is that Banda is ripe for social and political change. The Pink Gang could not have come at a better time to sow the seeds of this change.

Some sociologists have stated that in a corrupt environment, people have to take matters in their own hands. The Pink Gang should be a wake-up call to the politicians in the world's biggest democracy.

Chapter-40

Child Trafficking

Violence against children is one of the worst acts imaginable. As most of the world turns a blind eye to this problem, the incidence of violence continues to grow and it has now reached staggering proportions. According to a United Nations study of violence against children around, "40 million children are abused every year." The figures for sexual violence are even greater. The UN study points out that over 150 million girls and 73 million boys experience sexual violence and around two million children are actively involved in prostitution and pornography. What is alarming is that most of the violence is carried out by those who are close to children. They may include parents, neighbors and friends.

In the Asian subcontinent, the numbers are not only astounding but they bear the stamp of doom and tragedy. In Nepal, it is estimated that every year approximately 10,000 girls are trafficked against their wills and are sold in brothels in Mumbai and other cities. It is pointed out that "girl-trafficking today is a multi-billion dollar industry in Nepal. Among the biggest profiteers are the traffickers; whether syndicated professionals, greedy relatives, or so-called 'friends' who profit hugely from the practice." What is chilling to learn is that around 70 per cent of the girls in India's brothels are HIV-positive.

The estimate for the year 2010 show that nearly 20,000 Nepalese girls will be the victims of child trafficking across the Indian border. But India and Nepal are not the only countries in Asia to experience child-trafficking on a large scale. A number of surveys indicate that in the Mekong region of South East Asia, around 35 per cent of those who are trafficked are girls. In 2005, President George W Bush told the United Nations that child trafficking had become a top priority for his administration. The Secretary of State, Colin Powell, had a special office that was dedicated to the problem. In a wide-ranging interview with NBC television, Colin Powell said that child trafficking was the worst type of human exploitation imaginable. According to Mr Powell, "Can you imagine young children, learning their ABCs or whatever is equivalent in their language, being used as sexual slaves for predators? It is a sin against humanity, and it is a horrendous crime."

In order to see what was happening on the ground and to bring the problem to light, an NBC team visited Cambodia to record under-cover, the extent of the problem. The team found that it was easy to find young children who were sold for sex. The NBC team stated that there were "girls some so young they could be in kindergarten are for sale. Throughout the village, we see the same scene, at one brothel after another. Everyone here seems to know a little English, when they talk about sex, they use simple child-like terms anyone can understand." One of the setbacks that the NBC team reported was that arrests and prosecution were difficult if not impossible, given the fact that the police would turn a blind eye to the trade. It was not uncommon for the Police itself to have links in the sex trade involving children.

The example of child trafficking in Cambodia is just one of many cases of the abuse of children. When children are sold into slavery, a number of other cruelties take place. These could very well include prostitution and child pornography. What are the causes of child trafficking and why does more need to be done to stop this inhumane practice? One of the main causes is poverty. The possibility of earning lots of money can lead parents and relatives to push children into prostitution. The organization that advocates against the commercial sexual acts of children (CSEC) states, "Relatively high incomes, family dysfunction, a cultural obligation to help support the family or the need to earn money simply to survive are all factors that lead to child trafficking." Then there are additional reasons such as weak family structures, violence in the family, alcohol abuse or drug consumption. These can induce children to run away from their homes. When children are found in the streets, they become particularly vulnerable to the 'sharks' that pry on weaknesses.

Tourism, as was seen in the case of Cambodia, is another pull factor. Tourists from Western countries are known to frequent developing countries with the intention of exploiting children and this breeds its own supply and demand mechanisms. In Mongolia, women and children are trafficked into China, South Korea, Japan and Switzerland. Given the scope and severity of child trafficking and the devastating consequences it has on children, what can be done to combat and eliminate child trafficking?

The United States and other Western countries must take the lead and be in the forefront. These countries must provide information about the nature of child trafficking. The danger of the practice should be highlighted. Governments should work closely with non-governmental organizations to combat the problem. There is need for anti-trafficking legislation to be formulated and implemented. If those countries that are affected need help, then others can pitch in and offer assistance. The United States, for instance, has helped some countries to draft legislation and has also trained law enforcement officials and border patrol guards to detect traffickers. But clearly, more needs to be done. There are two areas in which attention should be drawn. The first is education and the second is rehabilitation.

The circulation of information is vital if child trafficking is to be stopped. The extent of the problem should be publicized in the media and on the internet. Government should be required to sign and ratify UN conventions to stop child trafficking and appropriate penalties should be imposed on governments that fail to carry out international mandates. But what about the victims of child-trafficking? There is need for local programs to be set up in countries to rehabilitate the victims. In Nepal, for instance, anti-child trafficking projects help train victims and provide microfinance schemes so that they can start businesses.

There is need for counseling, therapy, and income generating projects and the latter can be done on a group basis. As one representative in Nepal puts it, "We're helping them make most of their existing skills such as weaving, embroidery or making handicrafts. We are helping these children to develop new relevant professional skills, such as basic veterinary skills. Only with a regular income can they protect themselves against exploitation."

Chapter-41

Domestic Violence and Abuse

He hit her and blackened her eye
She struggled to understand the reason why
You see, she lived only for him
Thinking their lights would never go dim

Then one day he beat her again
This time she ran away in pain
And vowed never to take him back
She didn't want another attack

But he kept calling and begging
Her phone wouldn't stop ringing
She remembered the music and the dance
And decided to give him another chance

But one day he started another fight
Saying she couldn't do anything right
Now she lay crushed on the floor
Her laughter and beauty are no more

A woman is beaten every 15 seconds in the United States. Each year, around four million women experience some kind of physical abuse. Domestic violence is one of the leading causes of physical injury to women and contrary to popular beliefs, it occurs among all types of families. Recently, New Yorkers were made aware of two high profile cases involving a politician and a newscaster. Hiram Monserrate is a New York State Senator who is accused of slashing his girlfriend accidentally. The court found him not guilty of a felony but guilty of a misdemeanor assault that could land him in jail for up to a year.

In the court of public opinion, Monserrate is guilty of more than a misdemeanor. The State Senate has formed a committee to investigate all aspects of the case and their findings are awaited with interest. Then there is the case of former *New York 1 News* anchor, Dominic Carter. His wife Marilyn Carter filed court papers saying that Dominic was a wife beater. She described an incident in 2008 in which she claimed Dominic Carter "attacked her while sitting on the couch by punching her about the face area several times and grabbed her by the throat." There is also testimony on tape in which Marilyn Carter stated that her husband called her an assortment of names that included, "dumb, stupid, and the B-word".

The standard definition for spousal or domestic abuse is "when one person in an intimate relationship or marriage tries to dominate and control the other person. Domestic abuse that includes physical violence is called domestic violence." It must be pointed out that domestic violence does not only affect women. Men are also abused and may be embarrassed to ask for help. It is generally agreed, however, that domestic abuse is used for one purpose and that is to maintain control over the person who is abused. Psychologists and social workers point out that domestic violence occur within all age groups and cuts across social and economic status.

What are the warning signs of domestic abuse and how can we recognize a pattern? If a partner is feeling afraid, is being humiliated or yelled at, or avoids certain topics because of fear of angering the other person, an abusive relationship could be in the making. In addition, if the partner has an unpredictable temper, is excessively jealous, puts down the accomplishment of the other person, is controlling, limits access to money, threatens to take the children away, threatens to commit suicide if one party should leave and blames the other person for his or her own behavior, then urgent help is needed.

It has been established that physical abuse is just one form of abuse. The pictures of singing star Rihanna were plastered all over the media. Her face was battered to the point where it was almost unrecognizable. But it has been revealed that Rihanna also suffered from psychological abuse prior to her boy friend Chris Brown's physical attack on her. Emotional abuse undermines and ultimately destroys the self-esteem of the individual. They become dependent on their abusive partner that they may end up feeling worthless. Some of the symptoms of emotional abuse include intimidation, name calling, yelling and screaming, and constantly blaming the partner when things go wrong.

Take the case of John and Suzy. Their story illustrates much of what we are trying to establish regarding abuse. When they were in the Caribbean, John was in the habit of putting down Susie. By the time they had left for New York, he had become hypercritical. But

Susie was hopeful that by moving to New York, John might change. At first, everything seemed to go smoothly and Susie was happy. But after a while, John began to hang out with his friends. He would come home at all hours with his boys and wake up his wife to cook and entertain his friends. While she was cooking, John would take delight in taunting her to impress the others.

Suzy felt that maybe if she found a job, things might change. But first she had to get John's permission. After weeks of pleading, John finally allowed her to work. She found a job in a supermarket. John seemed pleased that Suzy was bringing in an income but he demanded that his meals should be served hot and on time. She had to be at home at 6 pm and if were held up in traffic or the trains were late that was no excuse. Once she was asked to fill in for a staff who had suddenly become ill. John was so upset that he slapped Suzy and accused her of having an affair with the boss. Suzy was forced to leave the job as he kept calling her and her boss and was trying to track their movements. In the end, Suzy managed to get to the precinct and report the matter. Today, Suzy has rebuilt her life. She is a confident young woman who passed her GED and went to college.

Suzy's example is by no means unique. The story might be different but the outcome is the same. Abusive relationships, for whatever reason, are intolerable. If you or someone you know is in an abusive relationship, there are steps you can take to get help. Remember, you are not alone and there are organizations that are willing to listen to you and to offer assistance. Domestic abuse and violence is illegal in all states. There are a number of practical steps that can be taken to prevent domestic abuse and you need to be familiar with some of them.

The most obvious is to confide in a friend or relative. You may be told that every relationship has disagreements. While this is true, domestic violence is not a disagreement. As we have seen, it is a pattern of behavior that is used to establish control over a partner that usually end up with one person physically or emotionally hurt. Once the signs of domestic violence have been observed, there a number of things a person can do to get help. The most obvious is to call 911. When this is done, the person should keep a record of the police or incident report. If it becomes necessary, medical attention should be sought, and if possible, photographs of injuries should be kept as well. There are times when the injured party will have to move out of the home to avoid further abuse and such a residence may very well be a shelter.

Chapter-42

Gendercide

The statistics cannot do justice to the suffering. According to the United Nations, at least one out of every three women has been beaten, coerced into sex, or otherwise abused in her lifetime. In addition, at least one million women are sold into prostitution every year. Domestic violence, honor killings, infanticides, and abortions constitute some of the most vicious attacks on women. In fact, some studies have concluded that domestic violence is the fourth leading cause of pre-mature death on the planet, other than diseases, hunger and wars.

These days, it is difficult being a woman. In some countries, they suffer most from the AIDS epidemic. In much of Africa, women have to combat diseases, hardships from the environment and militias to secure a meal for their children. Who can really understand how a mother feels when her baby is dying from malnutrition and starvation? But this is happening today in a world in which most of the resources are concentrated in the rich, industrialized countries.

The United Nations report on human rights for the year 2004 came to the conclusion that for Chad, a country in Africa, "there were frequent reports of killings. The militias indiscriminately attacked those who had not fled such as the elderly and disabled with a particular emphasis on men and boys." But Chad is not alone in being the victim of selected killings. The shame of the century must be the suffering of the people of Rwanda and Darfur.

As the international community is caught up in the web of semantics, people are dying in Darfur, the targets being women and children. When people are killed just because of their gender, the world needs to stand up and ask why reason is allowed to escape those in power.

Female infanticide, or femicide is prevalent in many Asian countries. The desire to get male children put females at a disadvantage, even before birth. China had a population boom before the introduction of a policy to restrict growth. Planners realized that unless measures are introduced to limit the number of children, the country would run out of space and resources. The hidden momentum of population growth would mean that in 50 years, China's population would be at an all time high. Restricting growth then, was a sensible option.

But there have been problems in the implementation of China's population policy. At first, it was thought that "two children" per family would solve the problem. However, it did not take long for the government to change its policy to one child per family. In a country where the preference is for sons, how does a girl child fare? There have been numerous reports of abortions of female children. The one child policy is also open to abuse. A recent report in the *New York Times* stated that families that are rich could journey to the cities, and have more than two children.

Population control has been likened to the chicken and egg

syndrome. Planners argue that a country needs more people for development but the converse is that too many people will impede development. What is the right balance? The answer to this question is far from clear since the quality of professionals will have a lot to do with development. Two examples may help to illustrate the case better. Singapore has been known for its rigid social policies. In the 70s, Prime Minister Lee Kuan Yew encouraged his countrymen to practice birth control policies.

These policies were so successful that 15 years later, the government was giving incentives to boost population growth. It was feared that a shortage of skilled workers would be harmful to the economy. In India, population growth is at an all time high. Policies aimed at curbing growth have not been successful. In agricultural areas, large families are seen as a blessing since children provide labor and sons bring in dowries.

The children's arm of the United Nations (UNICEF) has stated that nearly a million baby girls are aborted every year in India. The organization estimates that there are 7,000 fewer girls that are born in India every day because of sex-selective abortions. This would amount to more than two million "missing girls" a year. In India, there are laws banning the mechanisms that might reveal a baby's gender prior to birth. These would include the use of ultrasounds. However, it is not uncommon for doctors to hand out pink or blue sweets to families after an examination.

In some of India's villages, the loss of girls is felt heavily since they help families with housework. One mother puts it rather aptly when she says, "I wish I had a daughter. A woman feels awful without a daughter. Daughters help their mothers. It is sad. But there were miscarriages." The "miscarriages" this woman is referring to is selective abortion. What has been the official response to female feticide in India? The government has stated publicly that it is opposed to the practice. Indeed, the office of the health minister is adorned with notices, extolling the value of the girl child. One such notice reads, "a daughter brings complete happiness in your life".

Despite this lofty statement, officials from the Voluntary Health Association in Punjab think differently. They point out, "Sex-selection tests are considered a status symbol". In that area of India, families would rather eliminate their girl child in the womb, or neglect her when she's born. India's health minister has stated that the government is embarrassed about sex selection. Dr Anbumani Ramadoss has stated that his government is concerned about child sex ratios.

Although there is no major wand to solve female infanticide, there are practical steps that can be taken. The Prenatal Diagnostic Techniques (PNDT) Act banning sex-selective ultrasounds was passed in 1994, but it was only in March 2006 that a doctor was jailed for breaking the law. Many activists believe that the key is to crack down on the sale of ultrasound machines to quack doctors.

This recommendation is good for India as it is for other countries. What would also be effective is constant monitoring and auditing. Selective killings of girls is a crime. It leaves the world devoid of the richness and beauty of the girl child. This policy is so cruel and short-sighted that a host of problems will occur, including a shortage of labor and population, polyandry, and in the long run wars and pestilences. It is time for the international community to act and stop this cruelty.

Section-VIII

Love, Romance and Sex

Chapter-43

Why Marriages Fail?

The bride didn't have time to blush. Life was uncomplicated in those days. In an hour, she was to be carted off to a far-flung village, leaving forever the warm bosom of her family. Her mother tried to reinforce what the priest had said at the wedding. Mustering courage, the mother sat beside her teary daughter. She chose her words carefully. "Today you are leaving us. Our doors are always open. But the one to look after and protect you is your husband. Listen to him. When there are problems, talk to each other. Live well with your husband's family. You will have to rely on them. And don't forget to pray to God. He will be there for you in times of comfort and joy."

Introverted and demure, the bride absorbed every word of her mother's commandments. Many years have passed since that day. Today, that bride is living in New York City. Her seven children have done well. Her daughter Sarah is getting married in August 2007. As she prepares for the wedding, what advice can this wise woman give to aspiring married couples? What happened all those years since she left her mother's house?

The lady smiled as she talked. "I left my mother's house in 1952. My husband and I didn't know anything about anything but we were determined to make the marriage work. We did everything together and supported each other. We labored in the fields planting rice. I worked up to the day before my son was born. In those days, there were no midwives and visits for check-ups. You get pregnant, continue to work and wait for the child to be born. When I started having labor pains, my husband put me on his bicycle and we rode to the nearest nurse in total darkness."

This summer in New York weddings will occur on almost every block. According to statistics, only 50 per cent of those marriages will survive. More marriages mean busy work for divorce attorneys. Why is there such a high divorce rate in America? According to psychologists and relationship experts, there are certain basic rules that govern every successful marriage. These rules apply whether couples live in the dusty villages of the Caribbean or a bustling metropolis such as New York City.

There is no doubt that trust is the key to a lasting relationship. When both partners are comfortable in the knowledge that each will work to protect and foster the growth of the marriage, there is security. On many occasions, a wedding will take place amid great fanfare and at considerable expense. The bride and groom cannot take their eyes off each other. In the space of three short months, people would be shocked to learn that the couple were heading for the divorce attorneys. She would blame him for betraying her trust when he started to flirt with someone else. He would blame her for all ills imaginable.

Apart from trust, the number one reason why marriages fail is the lack of communication. During courtship, couples take pride in finishing each other's sentences. After about three years of marriage, the cracks begin to appear and prolonged silences become the villain. The old adage that one should kiss and make up before going to bed holds true in many cases. It is not good for differences to multiply to the point where they can become cancerous. The Biblical injunction that "all bitterness, wrath, evil-speaking, and malice be put away" can go a long way to restore marriages.

What about listening? Who is listening to each other? In today's society, both husbands and wives may be required to work to make ends meet. A recent survey found that spouses spend more time listening to those at the workplace than to each other at home. Women, whether they are employed or not, will appreciate every little help given by their husbands at home. These may include assisting with the garbage, or washing up the dishes. Those husbands who do should be commended.

Money has a habit of creating disputes even in the best of relationships. When finances are not discussed prior to tying the knot, it can become a major issue after marriage. Who will pay the rent or mortgage, or the food or entertainment bill? In some homes, the family income is pooled from which the bills are paid. In others, it's a fifty/fifty deal but arguably the ideal situation is for both parties to be involved in the financial affairs of the home.

Marriages are not perfect. Mistakes will be made by spouses. There are times when a simple apology can do wonders to repair or heal a broken relationship. However, 'sorry' can often be the most difficult word to say. It may be seen as a sign of weakness. Therapists point out that instead of saying "it's your fault it happened", it might be better if the statement is "I shouldn't have done what I did. I can understand why you feel that way." This is more acceptable than repaying insult with insult.

Cultural and religious differences have always posed a challenge to marriages. There is no recipe as to how these differences can be overcome. There is agreement that couples need to communicate and learn about each other's culture and customs before the wedding day. It is also recommended that the parents of differing cultures get to know each other ahead of time.

What has love got to do with it? There is the view that one should like the person before marriage and then grow to love him or her as the years roll by. Physical attraction is not love. When the heat and passion evaporate, one partner becomes a lump under the blanket occasionally rising for air. Is this the male of the species?

What is the definition of a good marriage? In a good marriage, the reception after the ceremony should be a small affair. Each year, the anniversary should be bigger and on the 50th year, a baseball stadium should be hired to invite those who have helped to make it work across the years. In reality, very few reach this landmark. But if every marriage is based on respect, tolerance and the avoidance of reckless words, more stadiums can be filled to celebrate our most sacred institution.

Chapter-44

Are Men Necessary?

During copulation, male Australian red neck spiders fight their way to be eaten alive. They pull rivals from the jaws of females and somersault into vicious fangs. Male brown rats force their way into roosts and help themselves to whatever females are available. Male chimpanzees also dominate females even though the latter have been known to bond together to fend off advances. Socio-biologists argue that these examples prove that females rarely get the chance to eliminate males. According to one scholar, "the world is patriarchal because male aggression makes for a winning reproductive strategy." This is all about to change. Lower order animals are getting the chance to witness a record-breaking advance in science. In the last few weeks, scientists have been able to create human sperm in a laboratory. This has prompted endless debates on the question, "Are men really necessary?"

Margaret Dowd asks this question in a book of the same name and received a surprising array of responses. The majority of them showed that it was women rather than men who were insecure with the idea that men might not be around. How could this happen? In Britain, scientists have grown human sperm and the arguments have revolved around issues of utility and bioethics. For example, artificial sperm could be injected into eggs, thereby allowing men who do not produce sperm to father children. In addition, sperm grown in the lab could potentially shed light into the causes of infertility and this can lead to innovative treatments and research.

Another use relates to the chemical composition of sperm cells. By understanding its genetic structure, pills can be made to boost fertility. The scientist who is in the forefront of making medical history is Professor Karim Nayernia. He works at Newcastle University in England and says that his ground-breaking technology "will one day be used to help infertile men to have children". Professor Nayernia argues that assisted reproduction has opened a new door and has led to a different scientific order "from anything we have seen before." Professor Nayernia has already used this technique to create baby mice using sperm created in the laboratory from mouse stem cells.

The creation of human sperm has tremendous implications for the future of science. It also raises profound bioethical questions. Professor Nayernia has stated that his discovery, "when viewed through a microscope, has heads and tails and swims like normal sperm." He is convinced that they would be capable of fertilizing eggs and creating babies. Professor Nayernia has applied for permission to "use some of the artificial sperm to fertilize eggs for research purposes." But there are bioethical questions and the debate has started in earnest.

Is human reproduction mere biological act? Some bioethicists argue that there are strong social, psychological, emotional and legal considerations that must be taken into account. It is here that humans differ from the red neck spiders, rats and chimpanzees, and other lower order animals. What is clear is that in the world of bioethics itself, there is hardly any agreement. For example, Ms Josephine Quintavalle, Director of Comment from Reproduction Ethics (Core Ethics), stated that she is in disagreement with the research because "perfectly viable human embryos have been destroyed in order to create sperm over which there will be huge questions of their healthiness and viability."

Ms Quintavalle describes further procedure as moral madness. To her, it's like faking one life in order to create another. But Dr John Harris, Professor of Bioethics at Manchester University, England, sees it differently. He states, "I don't see any problems with the use of synthetic or laboratory-produced sperm. They will initially be used to make discoveries about the way sperm are formed and how problems arise, and that will be beneficial. Eventually, it will be used to solve male infertility and that will be wholly beneficial. It seems that this is one of those examples where people are groping around for a problem and literally there isn't one."

Professor Pranela Rameshwar from the New Jersey School of Medicine points out that there are serious ethical questions to consider as well. She says, "Imagine there are cultured sperm in the clinic from embryonic stem cells that an individual perceive as ideal (blonde blue eyes etc). This could end up with a population of pooled genes. So what is the upshot of this method? In the case of a young person who might have cancer and undergo intensive therapy, perhaps one can harvest the person's stem cell before therapy for later use. The end result is that should be science handled ethically."

The comments from Professor Harris sound logical enough

but will they allay the fears of those who feel that we are playing God? If humankind has the technology to manipulate reproduction, could we create a master race, a perfect army for wars, or a group whose intelligence is prized and valued and weaknesses eliminated? Professor Nayernia says that he is not interested in creating humans in a dish. The technology, he says, will take another 10 years to be fully operational.

One of the more serious questions that has surfaced is the extent to which men will become either important or redundant in spermethics. If women can make babies by using lab-manufactured sperms, where does that leave men? Will he be left holding the baby literally or wouldn't he be around at all? When human babies are grown in a lab, isn't this reminiscent of Aldous Huxley's vision in *Brave New World*? What if men were to become obsolete only to be picked up by the women of the mythic Amazon? What kind of a world would we have if men were to be relegated to the dust bin?

Take war, for instance. A world of women would not be interested in the invasion of any country. One can envisage a women president sitting in front of a computer and telling her fellow world leaders to cut out the nonsense and work for world peace, while she does her nails. No wars, no fighting, no armies, and yes, no feeling of female inadequacy. If you mess up, there is always the lab! What about religion? It is quite possible that we won't hear these endless debates about priests being celibate as females will run the priesthood. They would also get that plum position in Rome but there won't be a repeat of Pope Joan.

Psychiatry will be replaced by empathy. The billion dollar cosmetic industry will collapse. Who will women dress to impress? Love songs will die and video games will be on the decline. Some biologists argue that with the new technology, it is quite conceivable that men can be wiped out from the planet. Normal reproduction creates males and females half the time. Reproduction between only two females would create only females. If the human population ever reaches a limit, the number of men can reach zero.

But men can take heart. Female fatherhood may be a long way off. The man who made the intelligent design isn't about to give it up as yet.

Chapter-45

The Sex Industry

Deep in the suburbs of Queens, New York City, a man was fingering his keyboard. The more he stared at his computer the greater was the realization that he was on to something off the beaten track. He could make a huge profit if he planned his steps with ingenuity. He began to type fast and furious and with an abandon that made the 'mouse' a metaphor for his wristy deftness. After several tries he found, in living color, the object of his search. He was going to organize a sex tour to Thailand, to Bangkok to be precise, as this paradise for lewd living, satisfying every whim and fetish.

The man from Queens marveled at how easy it was to assemble a group of perverts to a faraway city to indulge in a deviance that sells. His group had paid handsomely to consort with boy prostitutes in Bangkok. In a city where anything goes, and where the night and day is blurred only by the next twinkling neon, the sex industry is big business.

Today, sex sells but its not a term that is used in glossy advertisements on Fifth Avenue. Rather, it is the depraved, the sick, and the absolute disregard for human decency that has become the bane of the sex industry. But what drives it to the point that children are bought and sold into prostitution? The answer is undoubtedly money, the gateway to lavish consumption and the source of many evils.

The sex industry today involves a wide range of activities that truly boggle the mind. It consists of prostitution, phone sex, pornography, stripping, madaming, pimping, internet sites, and various advertisements in papers, including those who need a sugar daddy! There is little doubt that the sex industry is an assault on human dignity and decency. The stripper who attracts comments from patrons overstepping their mark, the performers for webcams who tricked themselves that they are not really in the streets but are getting their acting break are all contributing to this vile industry.

The television program *To catch a Predator* on MSNBC is most instructive. It shows how by using the internet, people are willing to journey for miles to meet with underage girls. When confronted by the producer, Chris Hansen, you hear all sorts of excuses from men who have made long journeys. There was a doctor who said he wanted to help a young lady with her homework. Then a man turned up with his five-year old son to meet a decoy just to find out how she was doing. And who could forget "crazytrini85" who turned up at a house completely naked!

These are just a few cases that have been exposed by the medium of television. But what about the thousands that go unreported and take place everyday in America and elsewhere? The internet is unregulated; it has no central control point or censorship. In short, the internet is out of control and cybersex, in all its horrid manifestations, will increase in the future, and so will violence against women.

Violence against women occur in different forms but the result is always the same. Physical and mental harm often lead to a loss of self-esteem and respect. Some prostitutes have argued, "Its my body, why shouldn't I be the one to decide how I use it?" This argument is hollow and unconvincing. The brutality and violence meted to women can hardly compensate for the money that prostitution generates. Lets face it, not all the endings are those of *Pretty Woman*.

The sex industry today touches every country from Albania to Zimbabwe. It is global in nature and some of its victims may never recover from the trauma. The US State Department states that there are more than one million children in the global sex trade every year. In Cambodia alone, there are about 100,000 women and children involved in the sex industry. The case of Suzy is most instructive. Suzy was only six-year old and looking forward to her first day of school. She was sold by her parents when she was five-year old for about $100. In the next months, Suzy became a commodity in the multi-million dollar ring.

She was passed from hand to hand and drugged to be submissive and compliant. In recent years, Cambodia has been a key point in sex trafficking. In a country where the poor live on 50 cents a day, women and children are driven to the sex industry by poverty. Luckily, Suzy was rescued by a former prostitute who now runs a shelter for exploited children in Cambodia.

A recent report by the International Labor Organization (ILO) has focused its attention on the global sex trade. The report points out that as many as 50, 000 women and children are smuggled into the United States each year. They are "inducted into the sex trade or domestic work," according to the report. But the United States is only a small part of the epidemic.

There are about 2,000 women from Kazakhstan who work in South Korea's sex industry. There are at present 200,000 girls in Thailand who are coerced to cater to professional sex tours for American and European operators, according to the International Organization for Migration. In today's society, it does not matter whether the country is Nepal, Bangladesh, Burma or Pakistan; the reality is that young girls are forced into prostitution. What about the Japanese? It is interesting to note that spending on prostitution in Japan is about equal to the nation's defense budget.

Those who organize the sex trade are a varied lot. They comprise the Japanese Yakuza, Chinese Triad, the Russian and Italian mafia, Latin American cartels, African warlords and American financiers. This level of involvement makes it extremely difficult to eliminate the practice. It is little wonder that the sex trade is being compared to the original global trade in flesh which is African slavery.

It is clear that the sex trade has reached a point that begs for action. We need to restore pride and dignity to our women urgently. There are a number of UN resolutions and conventions that denounce the trafficking of women but these are basically toothless. However, the international community has agreed that policies need to be implemented to free the two million children who are involved in the global commercial sex trade. The United States account for an estimated 25 per cent of child sex tourists worldwide. Consequently, the world is looking at the United States to enforce the Protect Act of 2003. That law makes it an offense for US citizens to engage in sexual activity abroad with a child under 18-year old. In addition to fear, shame and despair that are faced by many victims, there is also the incidence of HIV and AIDS which many victims have to life with on a daily basis.

There is urgent need for governments and non-government organizations (NGOs) to join forces to stamp out the sex trade. There are a number of practical ways in which this can be made possible. A media campaign to deter would-be sex tourists need to be intensified. Messages can be paced on billboards, on television, street signs, hotels, in-flight videos on airlines, the internet, on radios, and in magazines.

The force of law is also needed to bring criminals to justice and the law enforcement officials in various countries need to work together to make this happen, actively supported by their governments. Advocacy groups are essential to bring about the awareness of the problem as well.

Chapter-46

AIDS Alarm: 2008 Report

It has been described as a global disaster. There are 7,000 new infections every day, and to date there are 33 million people living with HIV/AIDS. An estimated 25 million persons have died from the disease and this will increase substantially in the next few years. At the Olympic Games in Beijing, 100,000 high quality condoms were made available to the athletes. They were given free of charge in health clinics. Messages of HIV presentation in different languages were also circulated. Athletes received flash sticks that include fact sheets on HIV. The organizers argued that they expected the athletes to be educated about the transmission of HIV and to pass on the information to their peers.

The 2008 Report on AIDS globally states that the world is making slow progress in the fight against the virus. In 2006, at the United Nations meeting on HIV/AIDS, it was decided that there would be universal access to information, prevention, treatment and support. A target date of 2010 was set to accomplish these goals. Today, however, the situation remains as bleak as ever. For example, for every two people who take antiretroviral drugs, another five would become infected.

At Beijing, the organizers argued that it was vital to target young people since the 15 to 24 age group account for about 45 per cent of all new infections. It is generally recognized that AIDS is a global epidemic. In the United States, people are living longer with the virus due to improved technology. It was said that at the end of 2007, over one million persons were reported with AIDS in the United States. A further breakdown of AIDS statistics suggests that about 50 per cent of those infected have died. In the early 1980s, most of the AIDS cases occurred among the white population. However, by 1996, it had increased more in the black population than in any other.

It is interesting to note that a report on the incidents of AIDS in the black community makes shocking predictions. In July 2008, the Black AIDS Institute published a report and concluded that "the AIDS epidemic among African Americans in some parts of the United States is as severe as in parts of Africa." The report entitled *Left Behind-Black America: A Neglected Priority in the Global AIDS* is intended to raise consciousness about the disease and also to remind people that AIDS is very much prevalent in different communities.

What else did the report say? Phil Wilson, a founder and CEO of the Black AIDS Institute, said that many people feel that AIDS is a black people disease. This is a misconception. However, Wilson points out that in Washington DC, more than 80 per cent of AIDS cases are among black people. AIDS also remains the leading cause of deaths among black women age 20-24 years. It is also the second leading cause of deaths among black men in the 35 to 44 age group.

In a recent *Black in America* documentary, it was pointed out that five per cent of the population of the greater Washington area is infected with HIV. This is comparable to the infected population of Uganda in South Africa. Perhaps the most damning indictment comes from the Black Institute when it sought to make comparisons between America and the African continent. The documentary states, "If black Americans make up their own country, AIDS would rank above Ethiopia, (420,000 to 1,300,000) and below Ivory Coast 750,000 in HIV population". It should be noted that both Ethiopia and the Ivory Coast are on the President's plan for receiving emergency AIDS relief.

Apart from the United States, what is the present state of AIDS in the rest of the world? In the Caribbean, the picture is far from rosy. The Caribbean has been described as the second most infected region in the world, apart from Africa. The effects of AIDS on the social and economic system of a country can be devastating. In Zambia, for example, a shortage of school teachers has resulted " because more teachers are dying of AIDS than can be trained to replace them."

The AIDS epidemic continues to spread in Asia as well. One of the reasons for this is that the infrastructure for an effective response is underdeveloped. In China, HIV prevalence was 82 per cent among injection drug users. In India, it was estimated that in 2000, there were about four million persons affected by the virus. Europe and Central Asia have also seen increased rates of infection. In December 2000, there 70,000 HIV cases reported in the Russian Federation, with Ukraine accounting for most of them.

Sub-Saharan Africa is the region of the world that is most affected by AIDS. The HIV epidemic was first reported in countries such as Uganda, Kenya and Tanzania. In 2000, about 26,000,000 persons were infected with the virus and about four million new cases occurred in Sub-Saharan Africa. In order to assess the impact of AIDS on national development, consider the case of Botswana. In this country, 35 per cent of the adult population is infected with HIV.

What is the status of HIV/AIDS in New York City? At the end of August 2008, the New York City Health Department released statistics on the virus. It was found that HIV is spreading in New York at three times the national rate. According to the city's report, "The city counted 72 residents newly infected with AIDS in 2006 for 100,000 people. Nationally, it was 23." The highlights of the Report for New York City are as follows: Men accounted for 76 per cent of all new infections and this is three times more than women. Blacks make up 46 per cent of new HIV infections, Hispanics 32 per cent and whites 22 per cent. Half of new infections occur among homosexuals and nearly 60 per cent of new infections occurred in New Yorkers between the ages of 30 and 50.

In Guyana, the health minister Dr Leslie Ramsammy launched a World Awareness Day in August 2000. He said that the goal was to ensure that "no new child will be born in the world with HIV" and challenged the leaders in Guyana to fight the virus. The Guyana Government plans to have a National Day of Testing on 21 November 2008. The main method of HIV transmission in Guyana and most Caribbean countries is through unprotected sex.

What are some of the ways in which transmission can be reduced? Testing is a good idea but this is no substitute for information and education. Sadly, in the budgets of many countries, education about HIV is miniscule. Public information is almost non-existent, and when this happens, countries run the risk-increased infections. There is need to begin a robust campaign in the school system and extend it countrywide with the involvement of all sections of the population.

Chapter-47

A Princess Falls from Grace

In 1986, it was all so different. On a bright summer's day in July, the royal train proceeded through Admiralty Arch and down The Mall. Thousands had assembled there and were waving flags, singing patriotic songs and having a jolly good time. Prince Andrew and Sarah Ferguson were pronounced husband and wife minutes earlier and were headed for the palace. It was a happy day for the couple and the public was prepared to ignore the niggling suspicions that there may be trouble later in the marriage. Sarah Ferguson described her relationship with Andrew as brilliant and said that "Andrew and I make a good team".

Even before their marriage, both parties were linked to relationships that would set the tone for future problems. Prince Andrew had a lengthy affair with socialite Koo Stark while Fergie had a live-in relationship with well-known racing driver, Paddy McNally. Fergie was invited to Windsor Castle in 1985 to a reception to celebrate the horse races at Royal Ascot. She met Prince Andrew, a romance developed, and a year later, Britain celebrated the 'wedding of the year.' It was not an official holiday but it felt like it.

On the day of the wedding, Britain's three television channels carried live pictures of the ceremony across the world. This larger than life event had only whetted the appetite of the public for more things royal. One will recall that the other major spectacle had occurred in 1982 when Prince Charles married Diana Spencer, a bride that was handpicked by the Queen Mother. In the case of Charles, there was the small matter of Camilla Parker Bowles, who was lurking behind the curtains. In royal circles, there is always someone 'in-waiting'!

It was long felt by the royal watchers that the family at SW1 was not much different from any other. In fact, the term 'dysfunctional' has been used on many occasions to describe the residents up The Mall. When cracks appeared between Charles and Diana, few people appeared surprised. In one of her interviews, Diana said that the media was partly to blame for the break up of her marriage. She said, "I realize that their attention would focus on our public and private lives... but I was not aware of how overwhelming that attention would become... and how it would affect my personal duties and my personal life."

Diana also complained that her marriage was 'crowded' because the other woman, Camilla, was making her presence felt. Such problems within the royal family were nothing new and they have been well documented. One would recall that King Edward gave up his throne to marry a twice-divorced American, Wallis Simpson. This resignation made it possible for Edward's brother George to succeed him. After he died, the present Queen Elizabeth became monarch in 1952. What about the other members of the royal family?

Princess Margaret, sweet and charming, had problems of her own. She must have been tired of walking in the footsteps of her elder sister Elizabeth that she made some bad decisions. First, she could not marry the person she really loved who was Peter Townsend. She ended up with Anthony Armstrong Jones (Lord Snowdown) instead. As years progressed, Margaret took up with a younger man, Roddy Llewellyn, and they both made the island of Mustique famous. Princess Anne too found that the man she picked, Captain Mark Phillips, was not after all the best choice. They divorced in 1992 amid salacious gossip that she had love letters from a commoner and that her husband was seeing a palace employee.

Long before Dodi Fayed, Princess Diana was linked to others. There was James Hewitt and a Pakistani doctor, Hasnat Khan. While Diana was seeing others, Prince Charles was busy cavorting with Camilla and their tapes became a national scandal when they were made public. Sarah Ferguson, this supposed breath of fresh air that the stuffy British needed, soon had Diana sneaking out of the palace and odd hours and painting the town red. Some watchers say that it was Fergie that led Diana astray.

In 1992, more bad news was in the offing. The Queen's favorite home, Windsor Castle, was in flames. The renovations were supposed to cost 100 million dollars. Who would pay? The British public was in no mood to cough up millions for the repairs. The Queen agreed to pay income tax and to open up Buckingham Palace to visitors for a fee. In the meantime, Charles and Di were growing further apart. When Diana visited the Taj Mahal, she was all alone. In 1996, the couple were divorced, and a year later, Diana was killed in an accident in Paris in the company of Dodi Fayed. The Queen hoped it would all go away quietly but the public affection for Diana caused the Queen to take to the airwaves and sing the praises of Diana. Charles was now free to marry Camilla which he did in 2005.

Sarah Ferguson, Duchess of York and a party girl, carried on thinking rather blissfully that money was flowing like the Thames. She had played her hand by negotiating a paltry sum as a divorce settlement so she can continue to use the Royal title and be friendly with the inner circle. But Fergie began to incur the wrath of the media and the public with her indiscretions. A series of photographs were published in British tabloids that showed Fergie cavorting with a tall Texan by a pool as he examined the structures of her toes!

Fergie launched herself into a series of commercials, becoming the spokesperson for some of them. She even once subbed for Larry King on CNN. But in 2006, things went awry. She put her savings into a vitamin company that went bankrupt. Fergie, however, wanted to live like the Queen. Can Fergie reinvent herself from this latest episode? She is making all the right statements but it may be too late. While watching 'Oprah', she said that she felt sorry for the person she was looking at. It turned out that she was looking at herself.

The lesson from the Fergie affair is that money or the lack of it can lead people to do desperate things. This is nothing new but living beyond one's means is bound to lead to a sense of desperation. It happens to many families who live on periodic paychecks but Fergie is a compulsive spender, and this time with the Royal Family closing in, she may find herself left in the cold.

Section-IX

Entertainment

Chapter-48

Michael Jackson: King of Pop

He defined a generation. His life was shrouded in conflicts, contradictions and confusion. It is hardly surprising that in death, it is difficult to unravel truth from fiction and fantasy from reality. The 70s and 80s belonged to Michael Jackson. When Berry Gordy from Motown asked the 'Jackson 5' to come up with three Number Ones to launch the group, they did even better. They gave him four Number Ones and took the musical world by storm. Michael Jackson, the lead singer, became public property. Later in life, he sought to shun the publicity he once craved but found that he couldn't do so without paying a heavy price. The world demanded to know every little detail of his life. Privacy became impossible. Michael Jackson was trapped by the very technology he had used to propel him to fame and stardom.

Michael Jackson was a person of many roles. In some of these, there remained controversies that his most ardent of fans will find difficult to understand. Did he need fame or recognition by dangling a baby from a hotel balcony? What was the motive there? As the world tried to make sense of some of his actions, Michael Jackson might have some mysteries still to unmask. His contribution to pop music is so great that Sir Paul McCartney was moved to write: "it was so sad and shocking. He was a massively talented boy-man with a gentle soul. His music will be remembered forever and my memories of our time together will be happy ones."

It was in the 70s that a phenomenon swept the music world. While the initial quest was the 'Jackson 5', Michael as a solo artist was extraordinary. His association with Quincy Jones resulted in three of the biggest albums of all time. They were "Off the Wall", "Thriller" and "Bad". The album that sent Michael into the realms of superstardom was "Thriller". Its catchy tunes and lyrics followed by wonderful and innovative dances and pyrotechnics took pop music to a new dimension. "Thriller" became the biggest selling album in history and is likely to remain so since music these days are downloaded from the internet. The *Guinness Book of World Records* estimates that "Thriller" has sold 65 million copies.

Michael's fame and fortune led to unusual life choices. It was one thing to have Bubbles as a pet chimpanzee touring the world but quite another to establish 'Neverland' for millions of visitors or to marry the daughter of Elvis Presley. But more was to follow and it was not at all pleasant. When allegations of child molestation hit the media, fans were shocked and outraged. In an interview with Martin Bashir on ABC television, Michael stated that sleeping next to a boy in his bed was totally harmless. While this may or may not have been the case, the fact is that the admission harmed Michael's image. An out of court settlement was made with the young man's family.

Michael Jackson had additional color and drama to his life and they were so unusual that they grabbed headlines. For example, he is the father of three children but there is endless speculation as to how they were conceived. Was it the doctor who was the sperm donor? Indeed, the mother of his last child is unknown. Then there was the manner in which children were dressed. For years, mask and veils covered their faces as if Michael didn't want the world to be close to the children. Art has a way of erasing scandals or at least to temporarily set them aside.

Michael Jackson in his red jacket, black shoes and curly hair doing the 'Moonwalk' became a captivating sight. In 1985, he showed that his songwriting ability was also on the mark. He teamed up with Lionel Richie and both of them wrote "We are the World". The song reached number one in United States. How shrewd was Michael as a businessman? In 1985, Paul McCartney said to him that one day the Beatles catalog might be worth a lot of money. Jackson outbid both McCartney and Yoko Ono to secure the rights of more than 250 Beatles songs that was worth millions.

As the years passed, and Jackson's behavior became erratic, the albums did not do so well. In addition, Michael Jackson's lavish lifestyle meant that he needed quick money to pay his debtors. According to one of his accountants, Michael had "an ongoing cash crisis that meant he was spending 20 to 30 million dollars a year more than he earned." Some reports stated that "millions of dollars were spent annually on plane charters, purchases of antiques and paintings. If you want to take a trip with an entourage of 15 to 20 persons, then that becomes quite expensive.

Michael Jackson was seeking solutions to his financial problems. He had agreed to do a series of concerts in London and up to 750,000 tickets were sold. While this would have made him money, it would also have taken a toll on his body. There were conflicting reports as to his physical condition to do the tour. There were photographs that showed him in robust health while some people said they were doctored to fuel sales. There were also differences regarding the last moments before his demise and rumors continue to swirl regarding his life.

In his autobiography, Michael recalled the beatings and abuse that he suffered at the hands at his father, Joe Jackson. Joe was a hard taskmaster and one way that Michael regained some of the lost childhood was by building 'Neverland', a Shangrila that offered escapism. Michael's face was easily the most recognizable in the world but he took pains to disfigure it. In the final moments, as they scrambled for help, there were mysteries yet to decipher. Some of them included his role as a father, the identity of the parent to his child, his medical history and prescription drugs and even his last will and testament.

What was the exact role of Dr Conrad Murray the doctor whose job was to be at the side of Michael? The death of Michael Jackson is sad and unfortunate. The lessons are many. When a person is in the public eye, the world thinks that he or she is public property. Paparazzi frenzy leaves little time for privacy. When unusual behaviors are added to the need for extreme privacy, the superstar becomes trapped by the same adoring public that he so badly craves.

Was Michael Jackson greater than Elvis Presley or the Beatles? He had close links to both. He outfoxed Paul McCartney for the Beatles songbook and was married to Lisa Marie, the daughter of Elvis. The King of Pop married the daughter of the King of Rock and Roll. Most people have a 'MJ' moment when the world stood still and when life was good. It may be 'Billy Jean' or the 'Moonwalk' but seldom can a song come close to the purity and innocence of 'Ben'. The loss was great and hopefully Michael Jackson will find peace at last.

Chapter-49

Is it Cricket?

In April 2008, a wonderful event took place in New York. It had history written all over it. Cricket was reintroduced formally in America. This time it was the schools that became the nursery for the second most played game in the world. At John Adams High School, students took to the field to play another team thus adding another beautiful game to the already rich tapestry that exists in the school system. It is fitting that John Adams High School should be associated with cricket. As one of the founding fathers, John Adams played cricket and is reputed to remark that if heads of cricket clubs could be called presidents, then why couldn't the head of the United States be called president?

Benjamin Franklin, who is the best president we ever had, brought over a copy of the Laws of Cricket from England to teach Americans the intricacies of the game. Cricket in the United States then had a very interesting history. There were many clubs in the United States and games were keenly followed. Cricket in Canada soon took root, and in 1840, the first international game took place between Canada and the United States at Bloomingdale Park in New York. There were over 10,000 fans at the game. That remains the oldest international contest on record.

It was not long after that tours were arranged by the US and one such was to welcome the West Indians. In 1886, West Indies had a successful tour of the US winning 12 out of 14 games. It was the turn of the US to tour the West Indies two years later. No one could have foreseen the drama that was to unfold. At Bourda, in Guyana, West Indies were bowled out for 19 runs in 18 overs, 13 of which were maidens. The US probably knew about 20/20 cricket long before it was invented! When did the West Indies make a similar low score? It was in 1969 when West Indies were bowled out by Ireland for 25 runs. The fast bowler Shillingford topscored with nine runs!

During its heyday, English and Australian teams toured North America, including the great Don Bradman who had a liking for a cricket ground in Canada. Cricket began a natural decline in America due to the lack of facilities, touring teams and the emergence of baseball as the national pastime. But in other parts of the world, cricket was firmly placed in the imagination of the people. West Indies lost the 1933 series in England and home games to England and Australia.

In 1950, the spin twins Ramadin and Valentine took West Indies cricket to dizzying heights. The nucleus of a great team was formed under Frank Worrell, as West Indies won their first victory against England at Lords. The Tied Test in Australia gave cricket a renewed fillip and it was rewarded with world record crowds in Australia. Rohan Kanhai batted with the pomposity of a prince while Gary Sobers was showing why he would become the world's greatest all rounder.

India, Pakistan, New Zealand,West Indies, Australia and England completed the cricket-playing nations. But there was South

Africa that had openly practiced apartheid and was seen as a pariah by the international community. In one memorable series in 1970, South Africa demolished the Australians and showed why the likes of Graham Pollock, Mike Proctor, Barry Richards, Eddie Barlow and Dennis Lindsay would have been world-beaters if they had played in another age.

West Indies won the 1963 and 1966 series in England and followed this with victories in 1968 against the Australians. By 1972, West Indies cricket had entered the doldrums. Kanhai was appointed captain of the tour to England in 1973. He set about instilling discipline in the team and led his team to victory against England. A revival of the fortunes started in West Indies cricket and Clive Lloyd was able to inspire and mould the team into a great unit. This was evidenced in the 1975 World Cup that West Indies won convincingly. West Indies won again in 1983 but the signs were starting to show that replacements were going to be needed to fill the void created by the great players. Viv Richards and Brian Lara would bring glory though the latter was not able to convert his talent to victories for West Indies. In the meantime, Australia, India and Pakistan were working to take over the mantle left by the West Indies.

India won the 1987 World Cup, followed by Pakistan and Sri Lanka and this added big incentives to those nations to pump money in the game. There can be no doubt that three events have occurred in cricket that have radically changed the game. The purists argue that the 50-over format has damaged the game but this is not necessarily true. Cricket is strong and perhaps flexible enough to handle this version of the game. The first injection of radicalism was done by Kerry Packer.

Cricket under floodlights, a white ball, and players in multi-colored clothing sent the message that the game had to catch up with the times. Packer also showed that cricketers needed money for their livelihood and his 'circus' took the cream of the players away from the traditional cricket boards. Indeed, West Indies sacked its leading players in 1978 after they signed for Packer with Alvin Kallicharran leading the team instead of Clive Lloyd.

The inventors of the latest competition the Twenty20 series could not have known what they were planning when they sat in their offices. There are those who argue that the Twenty20 form of the game has destroyed cricket. It is all razzmatazz, glitz and slogging. Every ball has to be hit for a six or the crowd would be displeased. Where does this leave the five-day test which can end in a long boring draw?

Test cricket, we are told, is what cricket is all about. It is a test of skills, stamina and strategy. The 50-over form is still acceptable and even the 40-over John Player League was accepted for a long time before it was scrapped. There is money in the Twenty20 format. This explains why Kapil Dev went about signing the top retirees like Brian Lara and others to form the Indian Cricket League. The Indian Board was slow to act on the potential of Twenty20 cricket but now it is on top of the game.

The Indian Board has formed the Indian Premier League with the big names of Bollywood involved. The Indian actor, Shahrukh Khan, has reportedly spent US$ 70 million in buying a franchise. Most of the current players have contracts with the Indian Premier League. Where does this leave Kapil Dev and his lot? Incidentally, when Shahrukh's team, the Knight Riders, played the Deccan Chargers, the game was spellbinding. It had all the drama of a great game of cricket. The game also came with cheerleaders and pompoms imported from the United States!

The final intrusion into cricket is money, tons of it. It has come from the Texan billionaire Sir Allen Stanford. He has recently met the bigwigs at Lords. Sir Allen is offering US$ 100 million to the winners of five Twenty20 games between England and West Indies next year. That amounts to 20 million dollars for 40 overs of cricket! When last did cricket see so much money? Allen would be happy to make an investment for over a five-year period. It is not a proposal that should be taken lightly.

Chapter-50

Ghana's Elegant Funerals

Ghana is obsessed with death. It has some of the finest coffin-makers in the world. The cost of Boateng's funeral was 10 times more than his wedding. He had saved up a lifetime for this big day and today they are burying him in a coffin of his choice. It is a replica of an Air Canada jumbo jet bedecked with wheels and windows. Why he would choose this particular contraption to make his exit becomes clear when it is realized that Boateng worked for that airline. Today, the coffins come in all shapes and sizes. They can be in the form of beer bottles, vegetables, fish or crabs or chickens. Recently, a taxi driver was buried in a car-shaped coffin. Talk about taking your job to the grave!

If the Ghanian funerary practice sounds like an ethnographic oddity or a quirk from the pages of anthropology, customs regarding the dead and afterlife have been around for a long time. These practices may appear bizarre but for those affected, they are poignant and rich in meaning. In Mexico, the first two days of November is especially significant. It is on those days that Mexicans remember the dead and the continuity of life. During the Day of the Dead, ceremonies there are grand celebrations during which the dead are welcomed into homes through incantations and prayers. Stories are told about the good deeds of the deceased and gravesites are decorated with flowers and religious amulets.

Parades and ritual chanting occur on the second day of November and family members give each other gifts. South Korea shows reverence for the ancestors by preparing food. This is done through the use of internet sites. South Korea is the most wired country in the world. The cost of buying ritual food is cheaper than preparing it. Then there is Madagascar. Here "placing and turning the dead" has a new meaning.

Every five to six years, there is the famadihana ceremony. A family member might get a dream that a deceased relative is feeling cold or is hungry. The deceased is then ritually exhumed and placed on top of the burial mound. New shrouds are bought and there is the ceremonial wrapping. The entire day is spent with the dead after they are placed in the coffins for another six years.

Hindus believe that the ancestors must be honored, and during certain times of the year, food and drink and prayers are set aside for the pitres. In Madagascar, it is expensive to exhume and clothe the dead in a country where the annual income is 900 dollars per annum. The same argument applies to Ghana. In the Ghanian Parliament, the Minority Leader stated in 2005 that his country "was investing in the dead rather than in the living. Ghana has gradually drifted towards a society of funeral lovers other than lovers of life."

In a recent funeral in Ghana, a 70-year old man was buried in a bird shaped coffin. It was hand-carved and had layers of different colors. The man left behind four wives and 20 grandchildren. On the day of his funeral, mourners dressed in expensive suits. As the band played, a procession walked through the streets, and a crowd soon joined them. There were occasional stops for liquor to be poured on the coffin. When the coffin was lowered in the ground, the unexpected happened. Professional mourners proceeded to smash the coffin to bits. This was done to prevent grave robbers.

At the home of the deceased, a grand celebration followed, including eating, drinking, and dancing. The more lavish the feast, the greater becomes the status of the deceased. The send-off takes on a dimension that is as important as life itself. What is the cost of such extravagance? In Ghana, more than half of the population live on one dollar a day and the funerals can easily cost up to $4,000. Another interesting twist to the funerals is that the longer the body stays in the fridge, the greater the cost, and with that comes prestige as well. The Ga king was on ice for four months, but the Dagbon king holds the record. He was on ice for a whopping four years!

In Ghana, the funeral preparation is elaborate and nothing is left to chance. When a death occurs, the community gears itself for the big day. Beer and liquor are bought, t-shirts and posters are printed and flyers are handed out. A cameraman is hired to record the proceedings. People do not have to know the deceased. They just show up at the party. Those who are close to the deceased are expected to make a contribution to cover expenses.

The pomp and pageantry of funerals in Ghana have become so costly that the government of Jerry Rawlings was forced to set up a commission to study its effects on Ghana's economic growth. Predictably, the government ran into criticisms. Local leaders pointed out that the ancestors have to be treated with respect. A university professor pointed out that "if you don't perform these rites properly, the passage to the ancestors or heaven becomes a little difficult for your soul." These rites are also affecting another area. The medical schools cannot get corpses to teach anatomy classes. It is difficult to convince Ghanians to give up their bodies for medical research.

Professor Aaron Lawson of the Ghana Medical School said that "we as Africans tend to love funerals very much. So instead of offering the body to science, we would like it to lie in state." Ghana's Minister of Health, Courage Quashigah, has also entered the discussion. Mr Quashigah has observed that Ghana is suffering from a "national craze for burial and funeral festivities" and that this is the most productive industry in Ghana.

The Health Minister has further argued that while other countries are working hard to decrease mortality Ghana has "a national thirst for funerals thus boosting the price of coffins and funeral fabrics." It should be pointed out that life expectancy in Ghana is only 57 years and infant mortality has increased to 68 per 1000 births. How can the craze for funerals be refined and reshaped to develop Ghana? There is no clear-cut answer to this question.

The impact of culture on development has long been the subject of many debates. As was seen in the case of Madagascar and Ghana tradition exerts a powerful influence on the ability of planners to implement change. This is perhaps no more startling than at a recent funeral in Ghana. Kofi and Sarah were two strangers who saw a funeral and went to the party. They fell in love and are now happily married. They are busy on weekends attending funerals.